SOTHEBY'S

ART AT AUCTION 1998–1999

First published in 1999 by
Sotheby's
34–35 New Bond Street
London W1A 2AA

Copyright © Sotheby's 1999

Sotheby's is a registered
trademark.

British Library Cataloguing in
Publication Data

A catalogue record for this
book is available from the
British Library.

ISBN 0–9622588–8–1

Project Editor Emma Lawson
Desk Editors Malcolm
Cossons, Kate Quarry
Associate Editor Renée du Pont
Harrison
Production Co-ordinator
Lucinda Blythe
Production Control Ken Adlard
Art Editors Sally Jeffery and
Beate Stöckert, Jeffery Design
Art Director Ruth Blacksell

Colour reproduction by Precise
Printed in Germany by
Mohndruck, Gütersloh

ENDPAPERS: The Library,
Château de Groussay, in a
contemporary photograph by
Cecil Beaton

HALF TITLE: Alberto
Giacometti, *La fôret: sept
figures et une tête*, inscribed *A.
Giacometti*, numbered *2/6* and
stamped with the foundry
mark *Alexis Rudier Fondeur,
Paris*, painted bronze, height
55.5 cm (217/8 in), New York
$7,482,500 (£4,489,500)
16.XI.98, from the Reader's
Digest Collection

FRONTISPIECE: Detail of a
painted tôle chandelier
mounted with Vincennes
porcelain flowers, Louis XV,
mid 18th century, height
approx 130 cm (4ft 31/4 in),
London £287,500 ($468,625)
11.III.99, from the Estate of the
late Giuseppe Rossi. The
proceeds of this sale benefited
the Scuola per Artigiani
Restauratori, Turin and other
humanitarian charities

TITLE PAGE: The *Credo* of
Charles V, in Latin and
Spanish, illuminated
manuscript on vellum with
contemporary jewelled and
enamelled binding, Spain,
second quarter of the 16th
century, each leaf 4.4 by 2.5 cm
(13/4 by 1 in), London £205,000
($325,950) 22.VI.99. Shown
actual size

THIS PAGE: Akseli Gallen-
Kallela, *Keitele*, signed and
dated *1905*, oil on canvas, 53 by
66 cm (203/4 by 26 in), London
£243,500 ($387,165) 28.VI.99.
This key work of Finnish
landscape painting set a world
auction record for the artist. It
is now on display in the
National Gallery, London

PAGE 191: Niki de Saint Phalle,
Lion, silver paper and painted
plaster, height 22 cm (85/8 in),
Tel Aviv $34,500 (£21,735)
8.IV.99. This is one of several
models for a series of large-
scale sculptures for the
Jerusalem Foundation project,
Noah's Ark Sculpture Park in
Jerusalem

PAGE 192: Abdur Rahaman
Chugtai, *Jahanara at the Taj*,
signed in Urdu, wash on paper,
54 by 38 cm (211/4 by 15 in),
London £40,000 ($63,600)
17.VI.99

CONTENTS

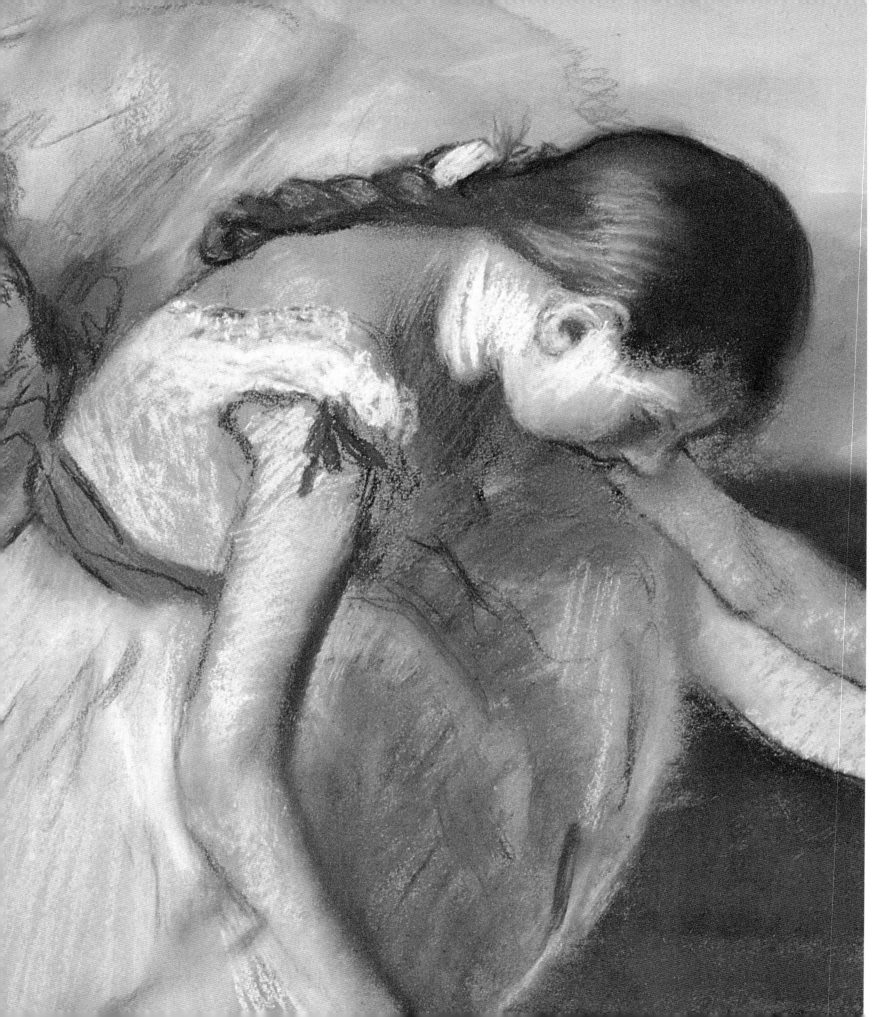

INTRODUCTION

Diana D. Brooks

In the early autumn of 1998, Sotheby's auction season held the promise of a series of milestones for the company. With the market continuing to expand internationally, some of the finest collections and works of art in the world were added to our sale calendars in New York, Europe and Asia. I am pleased to report that many of these sales exceeded our expectations, demonstrating the continued strength of the global auction market. These satisfying results, shown on the following pages, were particularly gratifying as they were achieved on the threshold of tremendous change for our company.

In the past year, three new buildings – in New York, Amsterdam and Zurich – have been the primary focus of our global expansion strategy, which will revolutionize the way we conduct business in the millennium. The most extensive project has been the construction of six additional storeys at our existing York Avenue facility in New York, which will open for business in September 1999. By the autumn of 2000, after the renovation of the existing four floors, we will have a brand new, ten-storey, state-of-the-art building which will become a major art, auction and cultural destination.

We think the Internet has profound implications for our business, and developing a strong Internet presence has been a key priority for us this year. Through our Internet business, Sotheby's and the over 3,400 dealers who are our Internet partners will offer exciting and authenticated property to millions of people around the world.

As always, it is the quality of the fine and decorative art that we offer that ultimately determines the strength of our business, and the 1998–99 season had many wonderful high points. World-record prices were achieved internationally in all of the major collecting fields, and several exceptional single-owner sales in both Europe and America made their mark on auction history.

Without question, the highlight of our New York auction season was the sale of Property from the Collection of Mr and Mrs John Hay Whitney. The Whitneys' superb taste is reflected on the cover of this year's *Art at Auction* with *Paysage, l'Ile de la Grande-Jatte* by Georges Seurat. In Europe we orchestrated the landmark sale of the contents of the famed Château de Groussay, which attracted 30,000 visitors and bidding from 26 countries.

Those sales are but two of the memorable auctions you will find on the following pages. As we go forward, providing our clients with an exceptional level of service remains our highest priority. We invite all of you to visit our wonderful new facilities around the world and to see us on sothebys.com, where you can experience first hand the dynamism of Sotheby's at this historic time.

Diana D. Brooks
is president and chief executive officer, Sotheby's

OPPOSITE *Danseuse au repos* (see pages 28–29, detail shown here) sold for £17,601,500 ($27,986,385) and set a world auction record for Degas. It is the highest price ever paid for a work on paper by any artist.

SOTHEBY'S YEAR IN EUROPE

Robin Woodhead and

Henry Wyndham

Recordbreaking results, unique collections, innovative events, all have added to the magic and drama of the 1998–99 season at Sotheby's Europe. Building upon the successes of the previous season, our salerooms across the continent have sold great works of art for unprecedented prices. A brief glimpse through the pages of this book reveal the extraordinary range, quality and rarity of items that have been sold at Sotheby's, evidence both of our specialists' expertise and commitment to their field, as well as our clients' passion for the objects they collect.

Yet Sotheby's is not just about the works of art and objects it sells, it is also about the places in which these items are sold. The face of Sotheby's in Europe is currently undergoing a transformation, both architecturally and structurally, with a formidable network of offices taking shape. The 1997–98 season saw the opening of state-of-the-art offices in Tel Aviv and the elegant new headquarters of Sotheby's Paris on the rue du Faubourg-St Honoré; now, in 1998–99 we were pleased to see the completion of London's dedicated Book Room, the renovation of the newly named Grosvenor Galleries (previously known as the Aeolian Hall) to house the rapidly growing Collectors department, and the opening of our new salerooms in Zurich. Relocation to the landmark Oberhaus, an architecturally important building in the Bauhaus style at the heart of the city's new art district, has enabled us

Possibly more than any other work in Yeats' oeuvre *The Wild Ones* exemplifies the artist's zest for life, here illustrated by a dancing man and horse. This painting achieved a new record for the artist when it sold for £1,233,500 ($1,998,270) in the Irish Sale.

Robin Woodhead is chief executive of Sotheby's Europe and executive vice president of Sotheby's Holdings, Inc.

Henry Wyndham is chairman of Sotheby's Europe.

to expand our sales schedule and provide a more comprehensive and efficient service for our clients. In Amsterdam work is almost complete on the new selling centre, which will have four salerooms and twice our current space. Opening in the autumn of 1999, Sotheby's Amsterdam will allow us to increase the number and variety of sales we offer and create a cultural destination for this expanding area of the city. These developments across Europe bear out Sotheby's commitment to change coupled with tradition, characteristics of a company with an esteemed 255-year history that has its eye firmly set on the future.

These guiding principles can also be seen in a number of events that took place through the year, which not only provided unique opportunities for interested buyers but also opened up the market to new clients. For example, in this summer's Asia Week bonsai trees were offered at auction in London for the first time in almost a century. These perfect living

studies in miniature, so suggestive of nature's struggle against the elements, brought a sense of wonder and calm to Bond Street's Colonnade Gallery, where they were on view. In contrast, the range of photographs, sculpture, paintings and drawings from Jean Pigozzi's Contemporary African Art Collection were a bright and electric addition to the Contemporary Art week at Sotheby's London in June. Until now this area of contemporary art has been virtually overlooked by the international art market, with Mr Pigozzi's Collection unrivalled throughout the world. The sale marked a watershed, with all but one lot selling, and many achieving prices well in excess of their estimates.

Yet perhaps the epitome of Sotheby's ability to combine experience with innovation this season was the sale of the contents of Château de Groussay, 2nd to 6th June 1999. Due to the continuing auctioneers' monopoly in France, Sotheby's was unable to hold the sale itself so, in an unprecedented move, it joined

Maintain Good Relations With Your Neighbours and They Will Help You When You Are In Trouble by Tanzanian artist Georges Lilanga Di Nyama was painted in 1992. It formed part of the Jean Pigozzi African Contemporary Art Collection and sold in London's summer Contemporary Art Week for £8,050 ($13,170).

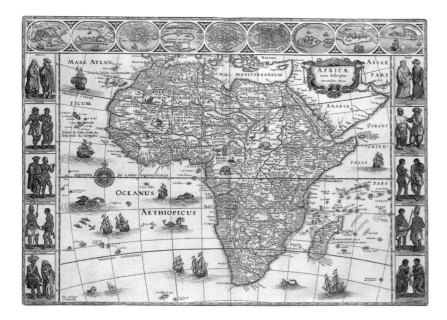

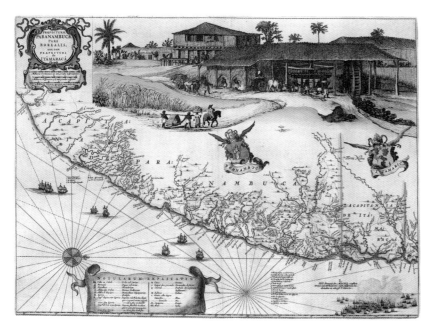

Le Grand Atlas, ou
Cosmographie Blaviane
(above) achieved a record for
a Blaeu atlas in March, when
it sold for £227,000
($370,010). In the December
Natural History, Atlases and
Travel sale a world map by
Giacomo Gastaldi, published

in Venice, 1546 – the first
edition of one of the most
influential maps of the 16th
century – made £146,700
($243,522): the highest price
paid at auction for a single
printed map.

forces with the Paris-based *commissaire priseur* Maîtres
Poulain et Le Fur. In this way, the most important
house sale in France for over 100 years was able to take
place on-site, keeping all the interiors untouched until
after the sale. Like many of the other extraordinary
single-owner collections offered at Sotheby's this
season, such as the Rothschild and Rosebery
Collection of Precious Objects (pages 36–37, 172), the
Rossi Collection of Decorative Arts (pages 34–35) and
the Ortiz-Patiño Collection of Books and Manuscripts
(pages 111, 114) to name a few, Groussay and its
contents were the embodiment of their owner's style,
passions and discernment. Opening up the house to
public view, many were able to see for the first time the
interiors created by Groussay's owner Charles de
Beistegui, which have exerted such an influence on
20th-century interior design. In her article on the sale
(pages 32–33), Laure de Beauvau Craon reveals the
extraordinary preparations required to host such an
event and, as she notes, it is often in such
circumstances that we see Sotheby's at its best. By
the close of the sale 97.7 per cent of the 2,070 lots had
been sold, achieving FF167,748,765 (£16,774,877;
$26,500,595), a total for such an event second only in
Europe to that made at the great Baden-Baden sale, 1993.

   Firsts were also seen this season in the range of
records achieved. The current state of the market has
shown that high prices will be paid for exceptional
works of art. Nowhere is this clearer than in the sale of
Degas's *Danseuse au repos* (pages 28–29), perhaps the
abiding single image of the season. Pictures of such
immaculate provenance, art historical importance and
visual power rarely come on to the market. To find a
comparable work by the artist one has to look back to
1983 when Sotheby's sold *L'attente* from the
Havermeyer Collection. *Danseuse* had been in the same
family collection for 114 years. It was still in its original
frame and had never travelled outside France, both of
which accounted for its perfect condition. In addition,
the ballet dancer is central to Degas's oeuvre and was
here rendered in an exquisite, and technically
accomplished, way – this was a truly great work of art.
Buyers agreed and, after fierce bidding, the pastel sold
for £17,601,500 ($27,986,385), setting a world auction
record for the artist and contributing to the highest
ever total for a Sotheby's London various-owner sale
of Impressionist and Modern art – £49.8 million
($79.1 million).

   Provenance, visual impact and freshness to the
market combined to make *Danseuse* irresistible.
Similarly this season, records were set for other works

This south German altarpiece, attributed to the anonymous 'Master of Rabenden', active between *c*. 1510 and *c*. 1530, sold at Sotheby's Amsterdam for Dfl 720,000 (£216,867; $352,941) in May 1999.

LEFT This Satsuki azalea was offered for sale during the June Asia Week in London. Bonsai are not valued for their age or size, but rather for their aesthetic appearance, which is influenced by the artist, who trims the shoots and removes or develops the branches.

RIGHT This rare Islamic gold filigree ring from the late 10th or early 11th century sold for £122,500 ($193,550) in July.

Felix Nussbaum's *Self Portrait with Apple Blossom* achieved a world record for the artist when it sold for $310,500 (£195,615) in Tel Aviv. Painted in 1939 when Nussbaum was in exile in Belgium, it reflects his questioning of his personal, artistic and political identity.

that fulfilled this criteria. In December's Contemporary Art sale, Gerhard Richter's seminal photo-painting, *Domplatz, Mailand* (page 90), Lucian Freud's major *Naked Portrait with Reflection* (page 95) and Piero Manzoni's archetypal *Achrome* (page 93) all set new artist records. Also in that month Sotheby's Zurich sale saw the low pre-sale estimate for Ferdinand Hodler's *Lake Silvaplana* (page 69) almost tripled when it sold for the recordbreaking SF4,182,400, an interest in Swiss art that continued to be seen in June's sale, with records set for Félix Vallotton and Edouard Vallet. These three considerations were also at play in May's Irish Sale, when Jack B. Yeats's *The Wild Ones* achieved a new record for the artist with £1,223,500 ($1,998,270), the third consecutive time Sotheby's has broken the record for a work by Yeats. With nine other artists' records set and the highest ever total for the Irish Sale of £5,744,847 ($9,306,652), this event continues to go from strength to strength.

Such results are not limited to the fine art categories; furniture, books, collectibles and the decorative arts have all seen exceptional prices for top-quality property and the pages of this book bear this out. Leafing through, readers may discover the former Spice Girl Geri Halliwell's Union Jack costume (page 184), a recently rediscovered 11th-century Islamic ivory box (page 120), a rare jacketed first edition of *The Wind in the Willows* (page 115) and two pairs of Italian carved giltwood sofas from the Collection of Count Volpi di Misurata (page 143), for example. It is this fascinating combination of disciplines, eras, styles, countries of origin and media that can make Sotheby's such a delightful place to work in and to visit.

Whilst *Art At Auction* provides a pleasurable opportunity to look back, a number of new and exciting events are already scheduled for the 1999–2000 season. We hope that you will take the opportunity to join us as we look forward to a new millennium.

SOTHEBY'S YEAR IN NORTH AMERICA

Richard E. Oldenburg
and William F. Ruprecht

Richard E. Oldenburg
(above) is chairman of
Sotheby's North and
South America. **William F.
Ruprecht** is executive vice
president and managing
director of Sotheby's
North and South America.

The happy combination of extraordinary works and a buoyant economy made 1998–99 a notably successful auction year at Sotheby's New York. In the autumn season of 1998, Impressionist, Modern and Contemporary sales generated the highest total at Sotheby's since the fabled height of the market in May 1990. The American Paintings sale in December set a new record total for our auctions in this category, and the October sale of Photographs was Sotheby's strongest auction to date in this expanding field.

Record levels continued to be achieved in 1999. The three-day series of Americana sales in January set a new high for this area at Sotheby's. May brought what was unquestionably the outstanding event of this auction year: the sale of Impressionist and Modern Art from the Collection of Mr and Mrs John Hay Whitney (pages 22–25). The evening auction on 10th May

Flag by Jasper Johns almost doubled its lower estimate of $500,000 to sell for $992,500 (£595,500). Executed in 1959 in graphite pencil and graphite wash, this is one of Johns's iconic interpretations of the American Flag.

LEFT *Captain Horatio Ross on 'Clinker' with Lord Kennedy's 'Radical' Ridden by Captain Douglas Beyond* by John E. Ferneley, Sr was commissioned in 1826 to commemorate Clinker's famous steeplechase victory over Radical. At $1,102,500 (£683,550) the painting achieved the highest price in the Celebration of the English Country House sale on 9th April 1999 and set a world auction record for the artist.

achieved $128 million (£78 million), far surpassing its high estimate of $95 million and setting new world records at auction for works by Cézanne, Seurat and Morisot. While soaring Impressionist prices naturally drew the most attention, excellent results were also achieved this year in other major areas such as Old Master Paintings, Jewellery, Antiquities, Latin American Art and African and Oceanic Art. New records were set in several specialized fields as diverse as Chinese snuff bottles, Byzantine coins, trophy silver and movie memorabilia.

However dramatic the record prices, the general auction market continued to be discriminating and selective, with most works fairly valued. The exceptional prices were appropriately paid for exceptional works, and the successes this year were primarily due to the very high quality of several distinguished single-owner collections which Sotheby's had the privilege of offering for sale. Prominent among these were the Whitney and the Reader's Digest Collections (pages 22–25 and pages 26–27), the Santa Anita Collection of Paintings by Sir Alfred Munnings (pages 30–31), and the Alberto Pinto Collection of Decorative and Fine Arts (page 42). Among many other notable single-owner collections, important works from the Masco Corporation were highlights of both the 19th-Century Paintings and the American Paintings sales in the autumn of 1998. Classic works by modern masters from the Morton G. Neumann Family Collection (page 84) were outstanding components of the November Impressionist and Modern sales. The auction in April

of rare daguerreotypes from the David Feigenbaum Collection produced yet another record-breaking sale of photographs (pages 40–41).

As always, the top lots in the wide spectrum of Sotheby's auction categories provide an illuminating overview of current collecting interests and valuations. In the November sales of Impressionist and Modern Art, 32 works achieved more than $1 million (£600,000). Modigliani's elegant *Portrait de Jeanne Hébuterne* (1919) from the Reader's Digest Collection set a new record for the artist at $15.1 million

BELOW Included in the sale of decorative arts from the Estate of Mrs John Hay Whitney, this mourning picture was embroidered by E. Ogden, a pupil at Lydia Royse's school in Hartford, Connecticut, and is dated 1813. Its pre-sale estimate of $30,000–40,000 bears little resemblance to the actual selling price, $167,500 (£103,850).

Afternoon Shadows by William Merritt Chase (1849–1916) achieved almost four times it high estimate when it sold for $673,500 (£424,305) at Sotheby's New York on 27th May 1999. It depicts Shinnecock, an area of beaches and dunes on the eastern end of Long Island, where the Chase family spent their summers.

(£9 million, page 26), and Picasso's early Cubist *Femme nue* (1909) from the Neumann Family Collection brought $11 million (£6.6 million, page 84).

The Contemporary Art sale in November achieved a strong total of $32.9 million (£19.7 million), with record prices for nine artists. Richard Diebenkorn's luminous *Horizon – Ocean View* (1959) from the Reader's Digest Collection provoked spirited bidding and brought $3.96 million (£2.37 million, page 27), nearly twice its high estimate.

The American Paintings sale in December achieved $44.6 million (£26.7 million), with new highs for 16 artists. Among the top lots were Mary Cassatt's delightful *Children Playing with a Cat* (1908) at $2.97 million (£1.78 million, page 75) and Frederic Remington's *The Belated Traveler* (1906) at $2.5 million (£1.5 million, page 73).

The sale of 19th-Century European Paintings in November brought a total of $20.4 million (£12.2 million). Several new records were set for artists at auction, including Bouguereau, whose allegorical *Alma Parens* (1883) sold for $2.64 million (£1.58 million, page 67). Despite some concerns about the regional economies, the sale of Latin American art in November achieved a solid total of $7.5 million (£4.5 million). While the top lot was Tamayo's *Still Life with Ice Cream and Melon* (1944) at $552,500 (£331,500), works by contemporary artists also sold well, with 12 new highs recorded.

In the Magnificent Jewellery auction in October, jewels from the Estate of Betsey Cushing Whitney brought $11.8 million (£6.9 million, pages 22–25), including $5.2 million (£3 million) for an extraordinary pair of blue and white diamond earclips by Cartier. The September Asia Week sales of art and furniture from China, India, Japan and Southeast Asia generated a total of $10.8 million (£6.3 million), including a record sale of Chinese snuff bottles from the Neal W. and Frances R. Hunter collection. The November French Furniture sale included two lots which sold for more than $2 million each: a Louis XVI porcelain-mounted table ($2.9 million; £1.7 million, page 144) and a baroque inlaid marble table top, perhaps the finest example of 17th-century *pietre dure* ever sold at auction ($2.75 million; £1.65 million, page 146). In the very successful African and Oceanic Art sale in November,

The five-foot high Mollenborg Horn, part of the Victor Niederhoffer Collection of Trophy and Presentation Silver, was made in Stockholm in 1897 by the court jewellers, Mollenborg, and was sold in December 1998 for $162,000 (£97,200).

which produced a total of $6.1 million (£3.6 million), two works brought more than $1 million each: a remarkable Kongo figure ($1.4 million; £859,500) and a stately, patriarchal Maori wood figure ($1.1 million; £661,500) the highest price to date for any work of Oceanic art.

The 1999 auction season was launched impressively with important sales in two major areas: Americana and Old Master Paintings. Coincidentally, the highlight in each of these sales was a rediscovered work of great aesthetic and historical significance. In Americana, this was a superb 18th-century secretary bookcase made in Newport around 1745 for the Reverend Nathaniel Appleton (page 21). In Old Master Paintings, it was a painting on copper by Nicolas Poussin, *The Agony in the Garden*, which resurfaced in the early 1990s, having previously been known only through contemporary 17th-century descriptions (page 20).

The Americana sale brought a record-breaking total of $20.9 million (£12.5 million), including $8.25 million (£4.9 million) for the Appleton secretary, the second highest price ever paid for American furniture at auction. The Old Master Paintings sale achieved

$31.3 million (£18.7 million), including $6.7 million (£4 million) for the Poussin, more than twice the previous record for this artist.

April brought a six-session auction of furniture and decorations from the Estate of Mrs John Hay Whitney, which generated $13 million (£8.1 million), almost twice its pre-sale estimate. Highlights of the sale included William Blake's *The First Book of Urizen*, one of eight known copies, and the only one still in private hands ($2.5 million; £1.57 million, see page 112).

The May Impressionist and Modern sales were, of course, dominated by the presence of the truly extraordinary paintings from the Whitney Collection. In a thrilling evening session, a large audience saw a sublime Cézanne still life, *Rideau, cruchon et compotier* (1893–94, page 22), bring $60.5 million (£36.9 million), a new world record for the artist at auction and the fourth highest price for any painting at auction. Seurat's serene *Paysage, I'Ile de la Grande-Jatte* (1884) set the second artist record of the evening at $35.2 million (£21.4 million, page 23), and Berthe Morisot's charming *Cache-cache*, at $3.8 million (£2.3 million, page 81), established the third. The evening was a testimony to the remarkable connoisseurship of Mr and Mrs Whitney, who together created one of the greatest art collections in America and, with immense generosity, gave the larger part of it to public museums.

While not reaching the Whitney heights, the subsequent evening sale of Impressionist and Modern works from other consignors produced a gratifying $55.5 million (£33.8 million). The top lot was an important painting from Monet's influential series of haystack studies, *Meule* (1891), which brought $11.9 million (£7.3 million, page 83). Other highlights were Monet's *Waterloo Bridge* (1903) at $9.3 million (£5.7 million), and a lyrical Renoir painting of a rose garden, *Les rosiers à Wargemont* (1879) at $6.1 million (£3.72 million), $2 million more than its high estimate.

The next evening sale of Contemporary Art achieved a strong total of over $25 million (£15.5 million). Among the top lots were Lucian Freud's *The Painter's Mother* (1982–84) at $3.3 million (£2 million) and Calder's wall-mounted sculpture *Constellation* (1943) at $1.98 million (£1.2 million, page 92), more than twice its high

ABOVE This limestone stele, carved in Thebes during the reign of Amenhotep III (c. 1390–1353 BC) was acquired by Englishman Edward Roger Pratt in 1833 or 1834, and was recently rediscovered in the family cellars. It achieved $398,500 (£235,115).

FAR RIGHT This 19th-century Kongo figure, measuring 1.21 m (47½ in) high, is a *Nkisi Nkondi* (literally 'thing that do thing') which has been described as 'multi-functional, serving as a representation of a chief, doctor, priest and judge all at one time'. The *Nkisi* is invoked by driving nails into the sculpture. It sold on 22nd November 1998 for $1.4 million (£859,500).

estimate. Andy Warhol's iconic *Marlon* (1966), from the Kraetz Collection, based on a still from the cult film *The Wild One*, brought $2.6 million (£1.6 million, page 94) after intense competition among eight bidders. In the course of the sale, several records were set for works by younger contemporary artists.

May concluded with a very successful American Paintings, Drawing and Sculpture sale which generated $29.2 million (£18.4 million), including $7.3 million (£4.6 million) achieved by a single-owner collection of Taos and Western paintings. The top lot, at $4.7 million (£2.9 million, page 70), was Frederic Edwin Church's large, masterly painting *To the Memory of Cole* (1848), a tribute to his teacher and mentor, Thomas Cole.

The spring sale of African and Oceanic Art, like the preceding autumn sale, confirmed the resurgent strength of this market with a total of $5.2 million (£3.3 million), including three works at new record prices. The evening sale of Latin American Art in June was marked by active bidding which produced a healthy total of $5.9 million (£3.7 million) with 12 new artist records. The Antiquities sale in June drew a large public and brought a handsome total of $6.4 million

(£3.9 million), well surpassing its high estimate. The enduring appeal of movie memorabilia was emphatically affirmed in the June Collectors' Carrousel auction with the sale of David O. Selznick's Oscar for *Gone With The Wind* as Best Picture of 1939. A duel between two telephone bidders quickly vaulted the price far beyond its high estimate of $300,000. Michael Jackson, identified as the successful bidder, acquired this icon of film history for $1.54 million (£956,350), the top price ever achieved by an item of Hollywood memorabilia.

As the spring season drew to a close, the sale of Fine Books and Manuscripts attracted special interest, offering important documents of American history as well as letters written by the reclusive author J.D. Salinger. Its highlight was a letter written by John Adams three days before the adoption of the Declaration of Independence and discussing the ongoing independence debate. Adams noted that a 'a free Constitution of civil Government, cannot be purchased at too dear a rate . . .' For the privilege of reading such moving words in a Founding Father's own hand, the successful bidder deemed $635,000 (£400,050, page 108) not too dear a rate.

Carlton C. Rochell, Jr

Carlton C. Rochell, Jr is senior vice president and managing director for China and Southeast Asia and worldwide head of Asian Art, Sotheby's.

Designs featuring chickens were a favourite of the Ming Emperor Chenghua, and the design of a cock and hen with chicks is not encountered on Chinese porcelain before the Chenghua period (1465–87).

For Sotheby's Hong Kong, 1998–99, which marked the 25th anniversary of Sotheby's sales in Asia, was an auspicious year, and we celebrated by moving our exhibitions to an exciting new venue at the Conrad International Hotel in Hong Kong. The change of location was well received by our clients, who attended the auctions and events in unprecedented numbers. The highlight of the autumn auctions was the sale of Eight Treasures from a Private Collection, which featured a remarkable group of Imperial porcelain, glass and jade of the Ming and Qing Dynasties. A highly important blue and white *meiping* from the Yongle period of the Ming Dynasty, which sold for HK$11,020,000 (£854,263; $1,423,772), was the top lot of the auction and also the oldest piece in the sale (page 124). Together, the eight lots fetched a total of HK$37,775,000 (£2,928,294; $4,880,490), proving that even in the struggling economic climate at the end of 1998 high-quality property fresh to the market was in great demand and sold successfully as a result.

When the spring auctions were held, with the Asian economy seemingly in recovery and the market more buoyant, the 50th sale season saw yet another auction record set. In addition, the sales were organized for the first time around Asia Week, an international event featuring lectures and exhibitions as well as auctions, which has previously met with great success in both London and New York, attracting clients from all over the world. Asia Week Hong Kong also saw Sotheby's first Young Collectors event, intended to cultivate a new generation of collectors, attended by several hundred people for cocktails and a private viewing of the upcoming sales.

The highlight of the spring auctions was the sale of a *doucai* 'chicken' cup from the Chenghua period of the Ming Dynasty. One of only three such cups now held in private hands, it is decorated with two sets of cockerels, hens and chicks with rocks, red peonies and yellow lilies. This highly desirable wine cup (above) realized HK$29,170,000 (£2,333,600; $3,768,733), setting a new world auction record for Chinese porcelain as well as achieving the highest price for any Chinese work of art ever sold in Hong Kong.

In 1998 Sotheby's made the strategic decision to sell

BELOW One of the ten leaves of *Landscapes* which show poems and illustrations by Shitao, an outstanding 17th-century painter. The album far outstripped its estimate when it sold for HK$5,960,000 (£476,800; $770,025).

BOTTOM *Majestic Waterfall* by Zhang Daqian achieved the highest price in the Fine Modern and Contemporary Chinese Paintings sale held on 26th April 1999 during Asia Week. This late painting sold for HK$1,450,000 (£116,000; $187,338).

RIGHT The form of these beautifully translucent earrings, showing ripe peas in their pods, refers to the abundance of wealth. The earrings sold on 28th April 1999 for HK$3,540,000 (£283,200; $457,364).

Classical Chinese Paintings in Hong Kong only, and the first Classical Paintings auction, which took place during Asia Week, was an enormous success. Five new auction records for artists were set in the top ten lots. The highest price was realized by *Landscapes* (left), an album of ten leaves by Shitao (1641–1707), which sold for HK$5,960,000 (£476,800; $770,025), more than double its high estimate of HK$2,800,000. The sale of Modern and Contemporary Chinese Paintings demonstrated the strength of this market, and works by the renowned and popular artist Zhang Daqian again sold well (left).

The sales of Important Watches and Wristwatches, Important Jewels and Magnificent Jadeite Jewels finished the Asia Week series in Hong Kong. Although watches and Western jewellery are relatively new auction categories in Hong Kong, they are currently the fastest-growing markets in Asia, and all three auctions saw keen bidding from both long-standing international collectors and newly participating Asian buyers. One of the highlights of the jadeite auction was an important pair of peapod pendant earrings (above), which sold for HK$3,540,000 (£283,200; $457,364), nearly twice its pre-sale estimate of HK$1,800,000–1,900,000.

The combined Asia Week Hong Kong auctions totalled more than HK$190,000,000 (£15,200,000; $24,547,803), an increase in sales of 56 per cent over the spring 1998 sales. In every category strong prices were realized for top-quality items, indicating that the art market in Asia is continuing to recover and strengthen.

George Wachter and
Christopher Apostle

THE AGONY IN THE GARDEN BY NICOLAS POUSSIN

The Agony in the Garden by Nicolas Poussin, oil on copper, 60.3 by 47 cm (23¾ by 18½ in).

George Wachter is executive vice president and head of Fine Art, Sotheby's New York; **Christopher Apostle** is senior vice president of the Old Master Paintings department, Sotheby's New York.

Rome in the late 1620s was the undisputed artistic capital of Europe; the legacies of Caravaggio and the Carracci family had taken firm root and the artistic programmes of the Roman aristocracy, both religious and secular, provided more than ample employment for numerous artists of the first calibre. It was in this fevered and highly competitive atmosphere that Nicolas Poussin painted his exquisite *The Agony in the Garden*.

Having arrived in Rome only a few years before, Poussin had almost immediate *entrée* into the highest echelons of the city's cultural élite, particularly due to his association with Cardinal Francesco Barberini (the nephew of the then reigning Pope Urban VIII) and his secretary, Cassiano dal Pozzo, himself a distinguished scholar and a discerning and influential patron of the arts. Barberini and dal Pozzo became two of Poussin's greatest early supporters, commissioning a number of large-scale works from him in the late 1620s. In contrast, *The Agony in the Garden* is a small-scale cabinet picture, to be admired by the connoisseur collector and his cultured guest. The fact that two versions of *The Agony in the Garden* exist, both painted on copper (otherwise unheard of in Poussin's oeuvre), both on the same intimate scale and both nocturnal scenes, is extraordinary. The other version, which differs somewhat from the present painting, was commissioned by dal Pozzo from the artist. The present copper appears in the Barberini inventories as early as 1655, and was either commissioned by dal Pozzo as a presentation piece to Cardinal Francesco, or was ordered by the prelate himself.

Poussin's treatment of *The Agony in the Garden* is one of the most poignant in art history. Mankind, as represented by the sleeping Apostles in the foreground, is unconscious of the magnitude of the event that is taking place just nearby. Poussin has used a shimmering and controlled light to pick out the figure of the kneeling Christ and to highlight the beautiful angels and innocent-looking putti, all of whom proffer gruesome instruments of the coming Passion; it is, as is always the case with Poussin's best work, a highly intellectual interpretation, relying on such paradoxes to elicit the contemplation of the viewer. None of the scene's emotional impact, however, is compromised but is, as a result, emphasized.

The last record of *The Agony in the Garden* was in the division of the Barberini Collection in 1811, and its reappearance on the art market after nearly two centuries was an unprecedented event. It is rare to find a painting whose exceptional beauty is matched by such high art-historical importance and extraordinary provenance. We were delighted, therefore, when the painting realized $6,712,500 (£4,094,625) against its pre-sale estimate of $3,000,000–4,000,000.

THE NATHANIEL APPLETON DESK-AND-BOOKCASE

Leslie Keno

The highlight of the New York 1998–99 auction season in the American Furniture department was the sale of the Appleton desk-and-bookcase for $8,252,500 (£4,951,500), the second highest price ever achieved for a piece of American furniture. According to family tradition, the desk was manufactured in the 1740s in Newport for the distinguished New England clergyman, Nathaniel Appleton (1693–1784), and had descended in his family for over 250 years, through an American diplomat who settled in France.

I had first heard of the desk some years ago, when a French antique dealer walked into Sotheby's in Paris to say that he had seen such an object in an apartment on the Right Bank. In the spring of 1998, the family contacted Sotheby's Paris office and invited me to inspect it in person. I flew over immediately and was greeted at the door by two distinguished French gentlemen who were direct descendants of Nathaniel Appleton. As I studied the desk, I was immediately impressed by the great unity of its design, particularly by how the profiles of the silver parrots' beaks on the lopers were echoed in the curving outlines of the bookcase shelves and dividers, and how the shape of the dome was reflected in the shells on the doors, finials and in the arched drawers of the writing desk. I stood there staring at the desk in awe – it was simply the most magnificent object I had ever seen.

Soon after the desk-and-bookcase arrived in New York, I discovered the signature of the Newport, Rhode Island cabinetmaker Christopher Townsend (1701–73/87), a patriarch of the esteemed Goddard-Townsend family of craftsmen. Exceptional for its craftsmanship and exotic 'plum pudding' mahogany primary and secondary woods, the desk also offers unique silver

The Nathaniel Appleton carved, silver-mounted plum-pudding mahogany dome-top secretary bookcase, by Christopher Townsend, Newport, Rhode Island, the mounts by Samuel Casey, 1730–50.

hardware stamped by Samuel Casey (1723–73), the South Kingstown, Rhode Island silversmith who was arrested for counterfeiting dollars in 1770 and later pardoned. Dealers and collectors of American antiques have talked of finding such a piece with silver hardware as one might speak of searching for the Holy Grail.

With its exceptional craftsmanship, extreme rarity, intact condition and direct history of descent, the Nathaniel Appleton desk-and-bookcase is an icon of American furniture. The importance of these factors is reflected in the sale price for the desk, to date the most expensive piece of furniture ever sold in Sotheby's 255-year history. Its discovery has forced us to redefine the way we look at 18th-century American furniture.

Leslie Keno is senior vice president and head of the American Furniture department, Sotheby's New York.

THE COLLECTIONS OF MR AND MRS JOHN HAY WHITNEY

Diana D. Brooks

Diana D. Brooks is president and chief executive officer, Sotheby's.

Among the memorable auctions that took place at Sotheby's this past auction season, the unquestionable highlight was the sale of Impressionist and Modern Art, Jewellery, Furniture, Decorative Art, Books and Manuscripts from the Collections of Mr and Mrs John Hay Whitney, among America's foremost collectors. The property sold at Sotheby's extended across virtually every collecting category and came from their residences in New York, London, Saratoga Springs, Georgia and, of course, from Greentree, their wonderful home on Long Island.

Masterpieces were on every wall of Greentree, beautiful furniture filled each room, and the atmosphere was inviting and welcoming. Objects everywhere captivated the eye, unique and remarkable in their own right, but always part of the background. They enhanced, improved and illuminated, but never substituted for what mattered most to Mrs Whitney –

close relationships and great conversation.

Our pre-sale exhibitions were designed to capture Greentree's special warmth and Mrs Whitney's elegance, style and exquisite taste. Collectors certainly responded enthusiastically at the sales, aware that this was the only opportunity to acquire something from the world-renowned collection. The sales brought $170 million (£105 million), the second highest total ever for a single-owner collection.

Many exciting moments stand out – from Cartier's fabulous blue and white diamond earclips (page 25), to William Blake's masterpiece, *The First Book of Urizen* (page 112) to Cézanne's great still life, *Rideau, cruchon et compotier* (below). What will be most lasting of these memories, however, will be the vision and joy of a rare collecting partnership, enriched over 40 years by love of art, shared interests, philanthropy and a devotion to each other.

Cézanne's *Rideau, cruchon et compotier, c.* 1893–94, sold for $60,502,500 (£36,906,525), the fourth highest price ever for a painting at auction and a new world auction record for the artist.

A world auction record was also set for a painting by Georges Seurat when *Paysage, l'Ile de la Grande-Jatte* achieved $35,202,500 (£21,473,525).

Impressionist and Modern Art Charles S. Moffett

Charles S. Moffett is co-chairman of Impressionist, Modern and Contemporary Art at Sotheby's.

On the evening of 10th May 1999 Sotheby's offered a selection of Impressionist and Modern Art from the extraordinary Collection of Mr and Mrs John Hay Whitney. The 50 lots included a fascinating mélange of paintings, sculptures and works on paper. Among the most important were Cézanne's *Rideau, cruchon et compotier*, c. 1893–94 (left); Seurat's *Paysage, l'Ile de la Grande-Jatte*, 1884 (cover and above); Picasso's *Le journal*, 1912, and *Nature morte à la bouteille de rhum*, 1914 (page 86); Berthe Morisot's *Cache-cache*, 1873 (page 81); and Courbet's *Le chien d'Ornans*, 1856. Throughout the sale there were works of exceptional quality, such as a remarkable drawing by Picasso of 1906 – *Etudes* (*Seated Female Nude and Other Sketches*) – and Henry Moore's superb small sculpture – *Reclining Figure Curved: Smooth*, 1976 – as well as lesser but very beautiful works of great interest and appeal.

Each lot in the sale reflected Mr and Mrs Whitney's unfailing ability to select and acquire works of art that were special, pleasing and of great merit. It was a collection that was made with passion, feeling and a careful regard for the complexities and subtleties that are the hallmarks of outstanding works of art. Indeed, it is by no means a coincidence that Mr and Mrs Whitney were the donors of some of the greatest Impressionist and Modern paintings in the collections of the Museum of Modern Art, the National Gallery of Art, and the Yale University Art Gallery.

Among the highlights of the sale was the Cézanne still life. The composition is one of the purest and most elegant in the artist's entire oeuvre. Throughout the painting one finds rhythms, connections, echoes and links woven together with line, colour and touch that interrelate like the notes, chords, melodies and harmonies of the greatest and most enduring music.

Also included in the sale was Seurat's *Paysage, L'Ile de la Grande-Jatte*. It is one of only a few great works by

Seurat that remained in private hands, and of course it relates directly to Seurat's renowned masterpiece in the Art Institute of Chicago, *Un dimanche à la Grande-Jatte*, 1884–86. Seurat exhibited it twice during his lifetime and clearly intended it to be seen as an independent work of art in its own right. It is imbued with an unforgettable sense of peacefulness and serenity, and is one of the most sublime Impressionist paintings to have appeared on the market in recent years.

The sale was one of most successful single-owner auctions that Sotheby's has ever held. All 50 lots were sold, and world record prices were established for paintings by Cézanne, Seurat and Morisot. As we approach the 21st century, collections of great Impressionist and early Modern works will become rarer and rarer, and the Whitney sale will be remembered as an exceptional moment in the history of the art market.

Decorative Arts   William Stahl

Beginning on the evening of 22nd April 1999 and continuing over the following three days, selections from the extraordinary Decorative Arts Collection of Mr and Mrs John Hay Whitney were dispersed at Sotheby's. The property was gathered from five locations – Beekman Place, New York; Greentree on Long Island; St James's Place in London; Saratoga Springs, New York and Thomasville, Georgia. The eclectic blend of furniture, silver, ceramics, textiles, pictures, books and manuscripts reflected the Whitneys' wide-ranging interests, diverse lifestyles and, in many instances, their wonderful sense of humour. The six-session sale was arranged in broad collecting categories – City Life, Country Life and Sporting Life – providing a unique glimpse into the lives of one of America's great collecting families.

There were many impressive highlights among the 1,500 lots. The item that elicited the fiercest competition among bidders was William Blake's *First Book of Urizen* (page 112), which sold for an astounding $2,532,500 (£1,570,150), an auction record price for a book by Blake. Printed by the artist in 1794, it contained 24 colour-printed etchings, exquisitely finished by hand. It was one of only eight copies of the book known to exist and the only one held in a private collection.

Horse racing was one of the Whitneys' many interests and their small but inspired sporting art collection reflected their love of this pursuit. During

their lives a beautiful watercolour by Sir Alfred J. Munnings hung in their Beekman Place apartment. In excellent condition, *Violet Munnings' Horse 'Chips' at Chantilly* sold for $739,500 (£458,490), the world record price for a watercolour by the artist.

Interestingly, the highest-selling piece of furniture in the sale was a slant-front desk of American manufacture. Signed by John Shearer of Martinsburg, West Virginia and dated 1818, this remarkable piece had been in storage for many years at the Whitney residence in Saratoga. Rare and previously undocumented, the desk sold for the record price of $123,500 (£76,570). Remarkably, it had survived the Civil War and was one of a very small number of pieces known to exist by this maker.

The sale also included a group of very fine English furniture collected when Mr Whitney was Ambassador to the Court of St James's in the 1950s. One of the most important items from among this group was an impressive George II mahogany library armchair featuring lion's mask terminals, its apron and legs all richly carved in the best late Palladian and early Rococo style.

American Folk Art was also well represented. Among the carvings, pictures and textiles, including an extremely fine mourning picture dated 1813 (page 14) and hooked rugs woven with animals, figures and Mattos, the collection featured an outstanding carving

The Living Room at Beekman Place, New York epitomized Mrs Whitney's innate sense of style.

William W. Stahl, Jr is executive vice president of American Furniture, Sotheby's New York.

of an American eagle – a favourite subject of Mrs Whitney's. The unusually large, painted figure was in excellent condition and carved by one of America's best-known itinerant artisans, Wilhelm Schimmel of Cumberland Valley, Pennsylvania.

This rich, diverse collection of objects, acquired with intelligence, care and amusement, will certainly be remembered as one of the great style sales of the 20th century.

This pair of Cartier earclips were the highlight of the sale of Jewellery from the Estate of Betsey Cushing Whitney.

Jewels John Block

The evening of 19th October 1998 will long be remembered by jewellery connoisseurs for the auction of Jewels from the Estate of Betsey Cushing Whitney. Containing 119 lots, the sale featured both jewels and objects of vertu lovingly selected by Jock Whitney for his wife Betsey. By the time the hammer had fallen on the last lot, the sale had exceeded its high estimate and achieved $11.8 million (£6.9 million), a fitting tribute to what would be recorded in history as the fifth highest total for a single-owner jewellery collection sold at auction.

Throughout their 40-year marriage, Jock Whitney chose extraordinarily beautiful jewels for his wife, surprising her with them on occasions such as her birthday, their wedding anniversary and Christmas. When making his selections, he exhibited a great sense of design and a natural understanding of colour. Before making his final decision, he would spend hours with the top jewellers of the day discussing design issues as well as the quality of the stones. Although the pieces in the collection were purchased from a variety of sources, his favourite jewellers were Tiffany, Van Cleef & Arpels, Verdura and Cartier. Ultimately, the unique elements of unusual design, texture and colour found in the pieces he purchased contributed greatly to the success of the jewels at auction.

The crowd that filled the sale room that night most likely knew that success was inevitable when lot 30, a Louis XV gold and enamel snuffbox decorated with colourful bouquets of flowers, exceeded its $25,000–30,000 pre-sale estimate and reached the astonishing price of $222,500 (£131,275). As the sale continued, many of the jewels achieved prices well above their high pre-sale estimates. An exquisite invisibly set ruby and diamond flower brooch by Verdura achieved $167,500 (£98,825, right), twice its pre-sale high estimate. A pair of 18-carat gold, diamond and Kashmir sapphire earclips by Schlumberger, Tiffany

& Co and a pair of Fancy Vivid Yellow diamond earclips by Van Cleef & Arpels, embellished in 1969 by Schlumberger, both achieved strong prices, fetching $222,500 and $827,500 respectively (£131,275 and £488,225). But without doubt, the star lot of the sale was Mrs Whitney's extraordinary pair of Fancy Vivid Blue and white diamond pendant earclips by Cartier (above). So clearly associated with her superb style, the earclips were sold for the exceptional price of $5,172,500 (£3,051,775). The blue diamond in the earclips was one of the most beautiful stones ever to come up for sale and was also the first stone in an international auction to be designated 'Vivid Blue' by the Gemological Institute of America.

The Whitney's extremely personal and romantic collection will be remembered by collectors for many reasons but, above all else, it will be remembered for its style and beauty, as well as for the superb taste that it reflected – a taste that was often well ahead of its time.

John D. Block is head of International Jewellery, Sotheby's North and South America.

Designed as a cluster of sweet peas, this brooch by Verdura is set with calibré-cut rubies and with pavé-set round and baguette diamonds.

Charles S. Moffett and
Warren P. Weitman, Jr

On 16th November 1998 Sotheby's was honoured to offer for sale the 37 most important Impressionist and Modern works in the Reader's Digest Collection. The Contemporary sale held the following evening included the Collection's extraordinary Richard Diebenkorn, *Horizon – Ocean View*, 1959 (opposite).

The Reader's Digest Collection of paintings, sculpture and works on paper was acquired with a deep appreciation for Impressionist, Post-Impressionist, Modern and Contemporary art. With an unerring eye for colour and light, Mrs Lila Acheson Wallace, who with her husband Dewitt founded Reader's Digest in 1922, began to collect works for the company in the early 1940s. During the course of more than four decades, she sought and acquired outstanding works by such masters as Bonnard, Cézanne, Chagall, Degas, Diebenkorn, Giacometti, Manet, Matisse, Modigliani, Monet, Renoir, Sisley, van Gogh and Vuillard. Her goal was to create a visually pleasing and stimulating work environment, but she also assembled one of the finest corporate collections in the world.

Among Mrs Wallace's greatest acquisitions were Cézanne's *L'Estaque vu à travers les pins*, *c.* 1882–85 (page 82); Monet's *Paysage dans l'Ile Saint-Martin*, 1881, and *Le bassin aux nymphéas*, 1917–19; Modigliani's *Portrait de Jeanne Hébuterne*, 1919 (left), and *Portrait de Jeanne Hébuterne assise dans un fauteuil*, 1918; Giacometti's *La fôret: sept figures et une tête*, 1950 (page 1); and Diebenkorn's *Horizon – Ocean View*, 1959. These works reflect the breadth and rich diversity of Mrs Wallace's interests, which extended from Impressionism to Contemporary art. The collection emphasized works imbued with colour and light, and the two paintings by Monet are among his finest. *Paysage dans l'Ile Saint-Martin* is one of Monet's most beautiful paintings from the 1880s. It combines the best attributes of his classic Impressionist style of the 1870s with the more experimental directions that he pursued during the 1880s. Complementing this

LEFT Offered in Sotheby's
Contemporary Art sale,
Horizon – Ocean View by
Richard Diebenkorn fetched
$3,962,500 (£2,377,500),
setting a new auction record
for the artist and bringing the
total for the sale of the
Reader's Digest Collection to
$90.5 million (£54.3 million).

OPPOSITE Painted in 1919,
Modigliani's portrait of his
mistress and muse Jeanne
Hébuterne was sold almost
80 years later for $15,127,500
(£9,076,500), achieving a
new world record price for
the artist at auction.

Charles S. Moffett
is co-chairman of
Impressionist, Modern
and Contemporary Art at
Sotheby's.

Warren P. Weitman, Jr
is vice chairman of
Sotheby's North and
South America and
director of international
business development.

exceptional work was Monet's *Le bassin aux nymphéas*
which employs vibrant brushwork and a rich palette of
blues, yellows and greens in celebration of the complex
play of light and reflections on the surface of his water-
lily pond in Giverny. This very important image was
especially appropriate to the collection because Mrs
Wallace played an important role in the restoration of
Monet's house and gardens in Giverny.

Another outstanding painting in the Reader's Digest
Collection was Cézanne's *L'Estaque vu à travers les pins*.
Analyzing the artist's work of this period, when he was
developing a new visual language, the renowned
Cézanne scholar John Rewald wrote, 'The difference
between the impressionistic sensation, which is rapid,
ephemeral and fleeting, and that of Cézanne is that his
sensations result logically in the full knowledge of the
subject in the classical sense. Cézanne often said that
he wished to "become classical again through nature,
that is to say through sensation".' In Cézanne's own
words, 'There are two things in the painter: the eye and
the brain. The two must cooperate; one must work for

the development of both, but as a painter: of the eye
through the outlook on nature, of the brain through the
logic of organized sensations that provide the means
of expression.' Moreover, in works such as *L'Estaque
vu à travers les pins* one is able to identify currents
and characteristics that created the foundations of
20th-century art.

Among the other highlights of this remarkable sale
were two portraits of Jeanne Hébuterne by Modigliani,
painted in 1918 and 1919. Of exceptionally high quality,
these images are enormously appealing. In the example
painted in 1919, the artist achieved a portrait of
extraordinary sensitivity, purity and elegance. It is a
subtle and deftly executed composition that combines
the influence of 16th- and 17th-century Mannerism with
the simplicity and exaggerations characteristic of the
best of early Modern painting. As such, it is typical of a
collection filled with images simultaneously pleasing to
the eye and imbued with the art-historical and aesthetic
significances that set the Reader's Digest Collection
apart from other corporate collections.

DEGAS'S DANCER

Andrew Strauss

Andrew Strauss, a senior director, is the head of Sotheby's Impressionist and Modern Art department in France.

An exquisite and luminous pastel of a ballet dancer by Edgar Degas was the star of our London summer 1999 sale of Impressionist and Modern Art. *Danseuse au repos,* widely considered to be the most beautiful Degas to come to the market in many years, sold for £17,601,500 ($27,810,370), setting a world auction record for Degas and the highest price ever paid for a work on paper by any artist.

The Degas had been hidden away in the Boivin family collection in Paris, figuring among the few remaining great works by the artist still in private hands. Virtually unknown to the outside world other than a few rare appearances at Degas exhibitions, the pastel had been preciously kept in pristine condition since its purchase in 1885, probably directly from the artist. These crucial factors certainly contributed to the success of its sale.

Jules-Emile Boivin was the co-founder of the French sugar company Sommier in 1869 and built the first sugar refinery in Paris. He was a passionate collector with an acute eye for quality, and his appreciation of the art of his contemporaries places him among the early French collectors of Impressionism. Through his friendship with Degas and Paul Durand-Ruel, who so successfully promoted the Impressionists, Boivin acquired no less than six important works by Degas, including the celebrated painting *La femme aux chrysanthèmes* of 1865 (now in the Metropolitan Museum of Art, New York) and a remarkable pastel, *Groupe de danseuses* of 1884–85 (Musée d'Orsay, Paris), recently acquired by the French Government from the Boivin family in lieu of tax. Another fine pastel from the Boivin collection, *Femme assise devant un piano* of 1882–85, depicting a woman reading a musical score, was sold by Sotheby's in 1999 at the same sale as *Danseuse au repos.*

Degas had an inherent love of music, and in the 1870s he began frequenting the Paris Opéra. Through friends, he was given unrestricted access to the entire building, including the rehearsal rooms, the stage and the dancers' dressing rooms. This special privilege, which he enjoyed for many years, allowed him to observe every aspect of the professional lives of the young dancers, many of whom came from poor backgrounds. He began painting ballet dancers on stage, either in full view of an audience or at rehearsals, but by the end of the 1870s started to focus his attention on capturing dancers off-stage in more informal and intimate settings. *Danseuse au repos* dates from *c.* 1879 and is one of the most beautiful examples from this series. Here, Degas portrays a seated young dancer resting on a bench, her tutu skirt billowing around her, highlighted by striking blue bows and pink stockings. From the relaxed position of her body, Degas conveys perfectly to the viewer her sense of physical exhaustion after the rigours of an intense dance and her absorption in her own thoughts.

Danseuse au repos is an outstanding work, and of particular note is the artist's highly complex technique. Degas used pastels moistened with steam and applied with a brush, further developing the areas around the dancer with gouache. Additional pastel colours were then applied in the traditional manner to highlight the dancer, creating a striking contrast of different media and a richly worked surface. Displayed in the original and very modern white box frame designed by the artist, this stunning image has universal appeal and led to considerable excitement in the days leading up to the sale. At the auction the bidding exceeded our pre-sale expectations within seconds. From then on, just two collectors were left to compete fiercely until the hammer went down.

The late grandson of Jules-Emile Boivin, who so graciously took pleasure in showing us the pastel, had met Degas on several occasions as a teenager and had enjoyed the unique pleasure of having the renowned painting *La femme aux chrysanthèmes* as well as *Danseuse au repos* hanging in his bedroom. It is extraordinary that a Degas of such immeasurable beauty and quality had remained in the same family collection since its purchase in 1885 and had never left Paris until this year, and the price achieved was a tribute to Jules-Emile Boivin's passion for Degas.

Rarely seen by the public until this year and greatly admired by all who were able to view this great work prior to the auction in London, *Danseuse au repos* made the Impressionist and Modern Art sale of summer 1999 a very special event.

THE SANTA ANITA COLLECTION OF PAINTINGS BY SIR ALFRED J. MUNNINGS

Nancy Harrison and
Benjamin Doller

Nancy Harrison and
Benjamin Doller are
co-directors of the
19th Century European
Paintings and Sculpture
department, Sotheby's
New York.

Why Weren't You Out Yesterday? captures the elegance, refinement and fashion of fox hunting so enjoyed by the artist and his wife.

On the evening of 1st December 1998, sporting enthusiasts gathered in New York at Sotheby's main saleroom to witness and participate in an unprecedented event. Ten highly important paintings from the Santa Anita Collection, all by Sir Alfred J. Munnings, were to be offered. Exhibited for years at the Los Angeles Turf Club, the paintings represented not only some of the finest examples of 20th-century thoroughbred art ever produced, but the opportunity to participate in what would become a record-breaking sale that would reaffirm the artist's well-deserved place in the history of sporting art.

Although by the hand of a British artist, the paintings carried with them a rare provenance inextricably tied to the history of thoroughbred racing in America. In 1934, two men, Dr Charles Henry Strub and the film producer Hal Roach, co-partners with a philosophy of providing top-notch racing in an incomparable setting, returned the sport of thoroughbred racing to California by opening the Santa Anita racetrack. Set against the

magnificent San Gabriel Mountains, the racetrack and its Spanish-inspired clubhouse immediately captured the attention of the public with its beautiful grandstand, formal gardens and English-style walking ring. In the years since its inception, Santa Anita has been the site of countless graded stakes races, as well as Olympic dressage and show-jumping events.

In 1950, Dr Strub set out to form a collection specifically for display in the Los Angeles Turf Club at Santa Anita Park. The paintings that he assembled, with the help of E. J. Rousuck of the New York art galleries Scott & Fowles and Wildenstein, included many of the finest examples of Munnings's work. From views of thoroughbreds taking their early morning exercise to the 'starts' at Newmarket and the winner's circle at Epsom, the collection covered the range of Munnings's genius.

The star lot of the sale, *Why Weren't You Out Yesterday?* (above), one of Munnings's favourite compositions, achieved $2,752,500 (£1,679,025), setting a new world record for the artist. The painting depicts two fashionable ladies in their well-cut habits, riding side-saddle, conversing with another smartly dressed lady on a hunt field. Munnings's wife and a friend posed for the painting, which also depicts four horses bred by Munnings himself. One of his most amusing and personal works, the painting was often referred to by the artist as a 'family portrait'.

The start of a race was known to hold the greatest fascination and inspiration for Munnings. Newmarket was undoubtedly his favourite racecourse and one that he visited frequently. *Under Starter's Orders, The Start, Newmarket* (right) is the quintessential Munnings canvas and one that portrays the excitement, tension and quick movements that contribute to the thrill of the start. The gleam of the horses' coats and the jockeys' brightly coloured silks are depicted in Munnings's impressionistic, bravura style. The painting was sold for $2,312,500 (£1,410,625), the second highest price of the evening.

The superb quality of *A Winner at Epsom* (right) was also appreciated by collectors attending the sale. The racecourse at Epsom was a constant source of inspiration for Munnings. In this composition, he not only depicts the victorious horse and jockey, but also provides the viewer with a glimpse of the groom, trainer and elegantly dressed spectators who surround the winners in their moment of glory.

Through the extensive research of scholar Lorian Peralta-Ramos, the curator for the Munnings exhibition planned for the year 2000 at the National Museum of Racing in Saratoga Springs, New York, each painting in the Santa Anita Collection proved to be interesting from both an historical and visual perspective. Whether capturing a specific phase of the race or depicting a stylish hunt in the countryside, Munnings's realistic attention to detail, his understanding of equine anatomy and movement and, perhaps most importantly, the emotion of the moment was evident in each painting offered from this unique collection. For the man who has been acknowledged as the greatest equine artist of the 20th century, new price levels were again recorded. It was, therefore, no surprise that the sale was 100 per cent sold, with every painting finding an enthusiastic buyer.

TOP The drama and excitement at the start of a race consistently fired Munnings's imagination. He wrote: 'Each start is a fresh picture for me, as they have been, meeting after meeting, year after year.'

ABOVE *A Winner at Epsom* was sold for $1,762,500 (£1,075,125) on the evening of 1st December 1998. The painting achieved immediate popularity and acclaim when it was first exhibited in 1955 at the Royal Academy, London.

CHATEAU DE GROUSSAY

Laure de Beauvau Craon

Laure de Beauvau Craon is deputy chairman of Sotheby's Europe and president of Sotheby's France.

When the gates of the park opened to a tide of visitors and the ballet of the helicopters began, I knew that Groussay would be a success – and what a success!

Yet the route had seemed strewn with obstacles since that day in autumn 1997 when we invited the press to a 'mystery tour' at an unknown destination, 50 kilometres from Paris. Few of the journalists arriving at the gates had heard of Château de Groussay or of Charles de Beistegui, and fewer still had visited that enchanting place previously open only to a select circle.

Built in 1815 at Montfort l'Amaury on the Ile de France for the Duchess de Charost, this magnificent property was bought by Charles de Beistegui in 1939. The heir to a fortune made in the silver mines of Mexico in the 19th century, Beistegui was attracted by the fact that the château was not classified as a historic monument, so allowing him complete freedom to transform it. From 1939 until his death in 1970, Charles de Beistegui, an interior designer of genius, worked with the architect–decorator Emilio Terry, enlarging and refurbishing the château and its gardens. Mixing mahogany, bronze and gilt-bronze, heavy fabric

The Library housed a collection of objects epitomizing Beistegui's eclectic taste.

and white piqué, English chintz and tartans, his innovations marked a new departure in taste. Following Beistegui's death, his nephew Juan preserved this mythical place carefully, and eventually asked Sotheby's to carry out an inventory.

We discovered some 10,000 objects, not only in the principal rooms and cupboards of the château, but also in the cellars, attics and even in the stables. It took months of work by a battalion of experts to catalogue and arrange the objects, thus deciphering the *goût Beistegui*, which brought together true works of art and copies, historic objects and modern creations with great freedom.

So the *goût Beistegui* was the trump card of the sale that took place from 2nd to 6th June 1999, which transformed the climate of the art market in France by becoming the most important house sale since the Revolution and the first sale held in France by Sotheby's in conjunction with a French *commissaire priseur*, Maître Poulain et Maître Le Fur. The arrangement caused a sensation in the media: the French auctioneers fulfilled the legal functions, while Sotheby's took care of the logistics and promotion of the event.

On the opening day 30,000 visitors queued to visit Groussay, strolling with astonishment and admiration through this reflection of Beistegui's imaginary world. The fact that each object was displayed in its original

context made the sale a great success and purchasers had the impression of acquiring a little of the taste of Beistegui himself.

While potential bidders walked the ground and first floors of Groussay, the cellars were transformed into a veritable bunker, equipped as if for a siege. A staff of 160 was assigned to carry out the kind of operation that has become a Sotheby's speciality: 10,000 bids from all over the world were registered by a tireless team of 30, linked to the rest of the world by 100 telephone lines, and, for the first time, potential purchasers could make a 'virtual' tour of Groussay on the Internet.

On 2nd June at 10.30 am the five-day sale began, and for over 50 hours Maître Poulain and Maître Le Fur took it in turns to wield the hammer. The sale was an enormous success not only financially (FF167,748,765; £16,774,877; $26,500,595), but also in the media attention it attracted.

So, 50 years after its creation, the Beistegui style epitomized by Groussay is once again at the forefront of fashion, not only amongst a small coterie as in the 1940s, but for a larger public, demonstrating how Beistegui's intuitive flair created a 'lifestyle' that was far ahead of its time. At the last sale, Juan de Beistegui declared, 'The five days of the sale have been a vivid homage to the work of Charles de Beistegui: the last celebration of Groussay.'

LEFT Lady Mosley remembered Beistegui as 'very Anglophile', reflected in the sporting note of the main entrance to the château.

RIGHT Beistegui turned the land surrounding the château into a *jardin anglais* with follies, including a pyramid, a Tartar tent and, here, a Chinese pagoda.

THE ROSSI COLLECTION

Mario Tavella

Mario Tavella is head of the Furniture division, Sotheby's Europe.

The pre-sale view of the Rossi Collection perfectly captured its decorative charm and impressive quality.

As the largest single-owner collection of furniture and related objects to come to auction in London for over 100 years, the Rossi Collection was certain to be a memorable event. Yet while the specialists had anticipated a good response from buyers, the results were even better than expected: the three-day sale achieved a total of £21,137,386 ($34,453,939), more than twice its pre-sale estimate.

The collection had been assembled with dedication and passion over a period of 40 years by the late Dottore Giuseppe Rossi (1914–79), a private collector and dealer from Turin, Italy. Travelling extensively for his work, Rossi was able to put together a comprehensive, and very personal, collection which would eventually form 1,400 lots, including 348 pieces of seat furniture, 308 painted and lacquered pieces, 138 gilt-bronze mounted objects, 32 commodes and 95 tables.

Yet Rossi's taste was by no means indiscriminate. He concentrated mainly on three regions of Italy: Venice, Genoa and Piedmont, while the proximity of the latter to France resulted in a broadening of the collection's scope to include a vast number of important French pieces. Dott. Rossi was also primarily interested in the furniture of the 18th century so that, with multiple examples in each category, the collection almost functions as a guide to the makers and styles of that period. That it includes numerous pieces with royal provenance will therefore come as no surprise.

Such characteristics would have been sufficient to attract buyers to the auction, but what made the collection so irresistible to many was its decorative quality. Nowhere was this more in evidence than at the pre-sale view: Rossi's preference for lacquer, veneer, precious woods, chinoiserie, ormolu mounts, rock crystal and porcelain flowers meant that for one week in March, Sotheby's New Bond Street galleries were transformed into the image of a Piedmontese royal residence. Filled with interested visitors, the view set the tone for the auction.

Beginning on the morning of 10th March with the session devoted to Italian furniture, this event swiftly gathered a pleasing momentum with its first 100 lots selling for a total of £3.8 million ($6.2 million). Amongst these was a tulipwood and ivory inlaid table (opposite) attributed to the Piedmontese cabinetmaker Pietro Piffetti, *Ebanista Reale* to Charles Emanuel III, King of Sardinia, and which Rossi had acquired from Umberto II, King of Italy in 1961; it now sold for £342,500 ($558,275), three times its high pre-sale estimate. Also fiercely fought over was a pair of

RIGHT This commode is stamped *M[athieu]. Criaerd*, one of a family of Flemish furniture makers based in Paris during the reign of Louis XV. In the 1740s, when this piece was made, Criaerd worked for the *marchand-mercier* Hébert, who supplied furniture to the *Garde-Meuble Royal*.

BELOW One of the many porcelain flowers included in the Rossi Collection.

RIGHT AND DETAIL
Pietro Piffetti was one of the most extraordinary virtuosi of the 18th century. His work is characterized by a fluidity of line in combination with great technical skill and lavish use of precious woods. The Savoy knots in this table indicate a royal commission.

commodes from the circle of Giuseppe Maria Bonzanigo that had been in the collection of King Carlo Alberto di Savoia; they achieved £315,000 ($513,450; estimate: £180,000–250,000).

Of the French furniture the most outstanding lot was an ormolu-mounted gilt and lacquered commode stamped *M. Criaerd* (above). It had been commissioned by duc de Luynes for Château de Dampierre in around 1740–45 and was in excellent condition; its price of

£397,500 ($647,925) was almost four times the low estimate. The highest price of the auction was achieved on the last day, when a large and important late Restauration, gilt-bronze mounted mahogany centre table of *c.* 1834, estimated at £100,000–150,000, was bought for £606,500 ($988,595).

Not all items in the collection were of this importance, yet there were interested buyers at all price levels, with a great many estimates being exceeded. For example, 24 porcelain flowers – so representative of the style of the collection – were estimated at £4,000–6,000; they sold for £23,000 ($37,490).

At the close of the last session, the collection was 98.63 per cent sold by value – a testament to Dott. Rossi's scholarship and taste. The accompanying four-volume catalogue, designed to serve as a future work of reference for collectors and students, was also a sell-out. That the proceeds were donated to charitable and humanitarian causes made the sale's success particularly pleasing. For, in accordance with Giuseppe Rossi's wishes, a number of organizations will benefit from the sale of his estate, including the Scuola per Artigiani Restauratori in Turin, which specializes in the conservation and restoration of 12 different categories of collecting art, providing young people with training to the highest international standards. And so Dott. Rossi's legacy of scholarship and dedication to the decorative arts continues into the next century.

PRECIOUS OBJECTS FROM THE ROTHSCHILD AND ROSEBERY COLLECTION, MENTMORE

James Miller

James Miller
is deputy chairman
of Sotheby's UK.

Securing the safety of an art collection is not a modern phenomenon. In 1855 when Baron Meyer de Rothschild, the first of his family to establish himself in what became 'Rothschild Country' (the vale of Aylesbury, north west of London), commissioned Joseph Paxton to design Mentmore, appropriate measures were taken to guard the growing collection of works of art. A vault was created beneath the Baron's room, entered by lifting the floorboards and descending a steep staircase. A bell would automatically sound in the Butler's Room in the adjacent wing, which was loud enough to alert the staff but distant enough not to disturb the intruder. Why such elaborate precautions? The short answer is a wondrous collection of silver-gilt objects: the passion of the Baron and one that was to be inherited by his son-in-law Archibald, 5th Earl of Rosebery.

This collection, displayed at Mentmore when the family was in residence until the mid-20th century, made no appearance in the great Mentmore sale, 1977. Its existence was only known through the catalogue of the Rothschild Collection written by the Baron's daughter Hannah, Countess of Rosebery. Last year Sotheby's was entrusted with its sale. From out of the 19th-century cases came cups, ewers, bowls, salvers, candlesticks, boxes, all testifying to the connoisseurship of Baron Meyer and his son-in-law.

and cost. He had been despatched in 1689 to engage the support of the Swiss in resisting Louis XIV's territorial expansion in Europe. And the City of Berne were to acquire the cup at the sale on 11th February 1999.

Six lots later, applause broke out in the saleroom as an agent acquired a silver-gilt ewer (left) which had been the subject of extensive research. When purchased by Lord Rosebery on 8th May 1893 it was noted in the invoice that the ewer dated from 1672 but bore the arms of William and Mary who did not come to the English throne until 1688. What had not been previously noticed were that the arms omitted those of Scotland, and the ewer was faintly inscribed on the bottom *Maundy*. It was therefore possible to prove that the ewer formed part of the Maundy plate used by William and Mary shortly after their succession to the English throne and before the Scottish Parliament had transferred its allegiance from James II to them. The applause did not erupt on account of this research, but because the purchaser was acting on behalf of the Dutch Government, and buying the piece for Het Loo, William and Mary's palace outside The Hague.

ABOVE This ewer, which fetched £199,500 ($325,185), was used by William and Mary in the observance of the Maundy Service.

The brilliant lustre of gold reflected from object to object: the paler gilt of the Augsburg cups, basins and ewers set in contrast with the rich honeyed tones of the salvers, casters and lidded cups of the Gorges Service. The ewer made in Naples in 1696 by a maker otherwise known only for the Baldachino in Troca Cathedral was the richest piece of all: the red tones reflecting in the swirls of its elaborate body. Some objects contributed to the warmth of gold against the coolness of silver, such as the pair of candlesticks by Albrecht von Horn, Augsburg 1650, where the stems in human form are cast in silver but loosely clad in gilt raiment.

The cataloguing of the collection took almost a year to prepare, drawing on the knowledge both of our Silver department and a range of scholars and family members. This brought dividends. The history of the Lion Drinking Cup (opposite), created by Emanuel Jenner of Berne *c.* 1690 for William III to present to the city's Äussere Stand and bought by Baron Meyer in 1860, was pieced together. The details of the original presentation were not clear. Information was gleaned from two inventories of 1791 and 1801 preserved in Switzerland, but the most important piece of the jigsaw came from the British Museum. Stored with the Blathwayt papers is a letter dated 10 June 1690 from Thomas Cox, William III's Envoy Extraordinary, where he gives details of the presentation

RIGHT The combined total for these 17th-century German silver-gilt beakers was £62,850 ($102,446), well in excess of their estimates.

OPPOSITE LEFT This magnificent Royal Lion Drinking Cup achieved a price of £507,500 ($827,225).

This was one of those rare sales that gave pleasure to everyone: the family trustees who were selling, the beneficiaries, the Silver department here and an enormous number of collectors and dealers who participated in the event. It will be a rare occasion when such a distinguished and well-chosen collection appears again on the market, giving the opportunity to so many to examine at first hand the masterpieces of the gold- and silversmiths.

One of the finest collections of period jewellery to appear at auction since the Second World War was sold at Sotheby's Geneva on 17th November 1998. It was assembled between the 1930s and the 1970s, and took its name from a spectacular creation by Van Cleef & Arpels, the Bird of Paradise brooch (right), made in 1942. This brooch, arguably one of the most famous bird ornaments in the history of jewellery, sold for SF487,500 (£211,038; $350,719), several times its estimate of SF135,000–170,000. Its bold design, sculptural quality and use of large gold surfaces in combination with calibré-cut rubies and sapphires makes it emblematic of jewellery design of the 1940s. At the same time it is a unique masterpiece because of its size, superb workmanship and perfect match of gemstones.

The collection has been compared to other great jewel collections of the period, notably those of the Duchess of Windsor and of Hélène Beaumont (see Sotheby's Geneva, 1987 and 1994), both of whom were part of the same social circle as the late owner. All three collections included important single-stone diamond rings of the whitest colour, although the example in this collection is the largest. The 58.61-carat Golconda-type stone (opposite page) could also be worn as an attachment to other items in the collection: a Van Cleef & Arpels knotted-ribbon brooch, which itself could be added to a magnificent diamond necklace by the same designer; or as a drop added to a Van Cleef & Arpels emerald and diamond necklace, which at auction doubled its low estimate (opposite page).

The emerald and diamond necklace is typical of the 1930s, when the most fashionable necklaces were designed as graduated collars of varying width, formed at the front by a festoon of gemstones gathered at each side in a knot or similar motif. A decorative element suspended from a clasp at the back – here the large

The collection, which totalled SF13 million (£5.6; $9.5 million) was named after this brooch by Van Cleef & Arpels, which fetched SF487,500 (£211,038; $350,719).

David Bennett is chairman of Sotheby's Switzerland and head of International Jewellery, Sotheby's Europe.

diamond – was another feature of these necklaces. The device was related to current dress fashion, as evening gowns of the period were designed to reveal the bare back. Naturally, jewellers seized the opportunity to adorn a hitherto neglected part of the body with drops, tassels and pendants.

A slightly smaller diamond (40.72 carats), mounted in platinum, proved to be the top lot of the sale, fetching SF3,303,500 (£1,430,086; $2,376,618). The stone could also be attached to a tassel of the Van Cleef & Arpels knotted-ribbon brooch, which could also form part of a dramatic necklace. The concept of multi-functional jewels was popular throughout the 19th century, and seems to have appealed especially to the

jewellers of the 1920s and 1930s. This particular combination, designed in 1949, takes the concept to the extreme.

The late owner of the collection was consulted personally by Louis Arpels, and was thus involved in the selection of stones and the design, so that the collection itself became an expression of individual taste, a rare thing indeed today. It is this element that added an extra excitement to what, judged by any criteria, was already a superb collection of jewellery: the feeling that one was not just looking at great workmanship and design coupled with fine-quality gems, but also that one had lifted a corner of the curtain over the past.

The largest diamond in the collection, which sold as a ring for SF3,193,500 (£1,382,467; $2,297,482), could also be worn as a drop with the emerald and diamond necklace, which sold for SF410,000 (£177,489; $294,964).

PHOTOGRAPHS AT SOTHEBY'S

Denise Bethel

Denise Bethel is head of the Photographs department, Sotheby's New York.

This whole-plate cloud study, which sold for $354,500 (£219,790), is strikingly modern in its composition, and maybe the only surviving daguerreotype of clouds by Southworth & Hawes.

On 27th April 1999, Sotheby's New York offered the David Feigenbaum Collection of Southworth & Hawes and Other 19th-Century Photographs, the most successful auction in the history of the photographs market. Never has such a small number of photographs brought such a high sale total: 111 lots fetched over $3.3 million (£2 million) and only one lot went unsold. This private collection, the most valuable ever sold in the United States, represents a watershed in the market, reflecting a wave of unprecedented international interest in this burgeoning field. The Feigenbaum Collection, combined with Sotheby's various-owners sale the following day, produced a grand total of $6.4 million (£3.9 million), a world record for photographs sold at auction in a single season. One week later, Sotheby's London held its most successful various-owners sale ever: in this £1.3 million ($2.1 million) auction the record for a Moholy-Nagy photograph sold at auction was almost tripled, when his photogram of a hand soared to £166,500 ($271,395, page 101).

The David Feigenbaum Collection displayed all the hallmarks of success: a hitherto unknown body of work by masters of their medium, brought to light at a time when serious photograph buyers are searching for fresh, blue-chip material. Albert Sands Southworth (1811–94) and Josiah Johnson Hawes (1808–1901) were among the finest daguerreotypists the world has known, and their stunning whole-plate portraits and

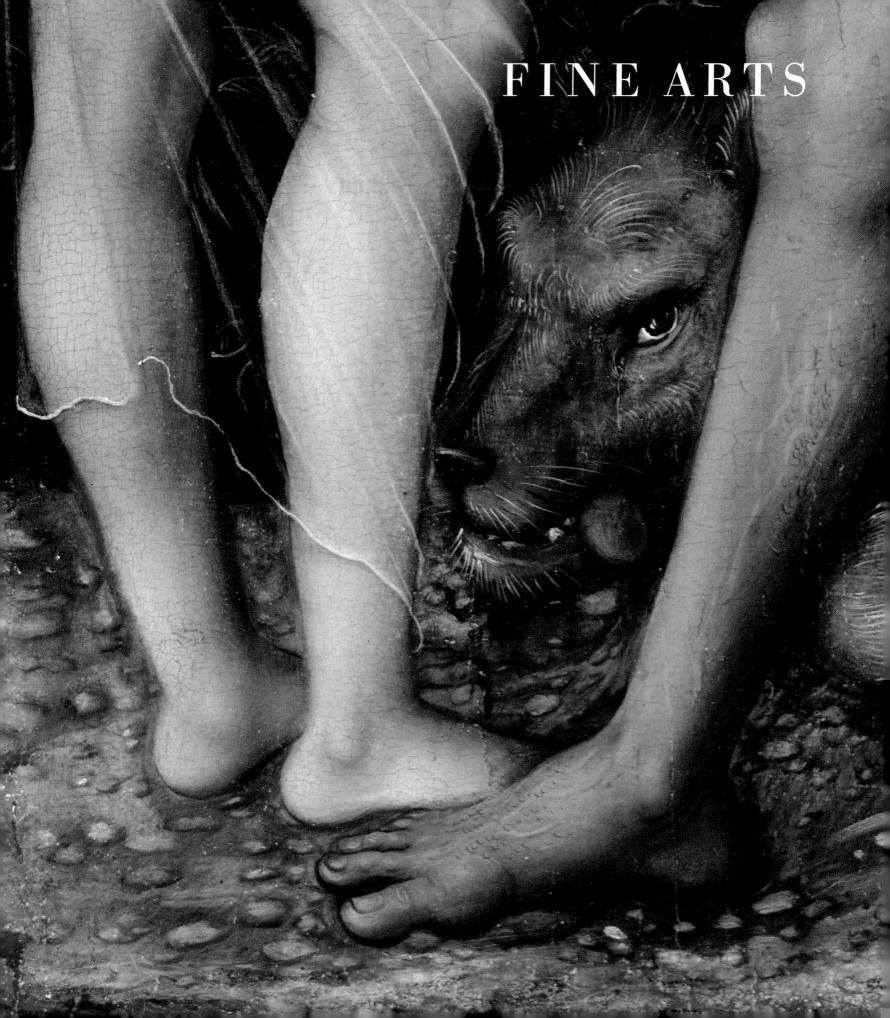

FINE ARTS

OLD MASTER PAINTINGS

Pieter Brueghel the Younger

The Triumph of Death
Signed and dated
P Brevghel 1626
Oil on canvas, 116.8 by
167 cm (46 by 65¾ in)
New York $2,037,500
(£1,242,875) 28.1.99
Property from the Estate of
Peter Putnam, Cleveland,
Ohio, sold to benefit the
Mildred Andrews Charitable
Fund

Pieter Brueghel the Younger
painted four versions of this
subject, but the present
example is the only one to be
signed and dated. It is a
variation of an original
painting by his father, Pieter
Brueghel the Elder, although
it seems likely, from
differences in colour and
detail, that the son had never
seen his father's original.
This ominous vision of
Death's work may also serve

as a memorial for the
Brueghel family, as it appears
to commemorate the life of
Pieter the Elder in the small
funeral banners that carry the
date 1526, the probable year
of his birth, and the Latin
inscription *obitt mortem*,
'he has passed on'. In
addition, it was painted in
1626, the year after Pieter
the Younger's brother Jan
and his three children died
of the plague.

Lucas Cranach the Elder
The Choice of Hercules
Signed with the artist's
device of a winged dragon
Oil on beechwood panel,
63.4 by 45.4 cm (25 by 18 in)
London £1,596,500
($2,682,120) 17.XII.98

This painting shows the
18-year-old Hercules having
killed a lion while tending his
cattle on Mount Cithaeron
and being visited by Pleasure
and Virtue. Hercules
subsequently rejects
Pleasure's promise of a life of
enjoyment, choosing Virtue's
path of toil and glory. The
allegory was popular at the
time, and Cranach would
probably have been familiar
with it from Sebastian
Brant's satire *Das
Narrenschiff* (1494) and,
perhaps, Brant's play
Hercules am Scheideweg
(*Hercules at the Crossroads*,
1512). The painting is a
mature work, executed after
1537, but is free from the
workshop intervention that
has diminished other
paintings of Cranach's
later years.

Jean-Baptiste Greuze
Cimon and Pero:
'Roman Charity'
Oil on canvas, 62.9 by
79.4 cm (24¾ by 31¼ in)
New York $178,500
(£112,455) 28.v.99

'*Roman Charity*' probably
dates from around 1767,
when Greuze began to
experiment with new subject
matter. Famous for his genre
paintings, Greuze began to
produce history paintings,
which were at the pinnacle of
the established artistic
hierarchy. This work is a
major rediscovery – reflected

by the price achieved, which
was nearly six times its high
estimate – and was
previously only recorded
through an ink-wash sketch
now in the Louvre. It appears
to be an oil sketch for a larger
work, which was never
painted, and shows Cimon,
who had been convicted of a
capital offence and was

being starved by his gaolers,
being visited by his daughter
Pero, who kept him alive by
suckling him. The story,
exemplifying the virtue of
filial piety, was popular with
history painters, and had
been treated by many artists,
including Rubens and
Murillo.

Jean-Baptiste Siméon Chardin
Still Life
Signed *Chardin*
Oil on canvas, 33 by 40.6 cm (13 by 16 in)
New York $525,000 (£330,750) 28.v.99
Property from the Collection of Mr and Mrs John Hay Whitney

The apparently simple composition of this painting conceals a sophisticated and balanced arrangement of almost only rounded objects – eggs, jugs, a copper pot and a pot cover resting on a circular stone ledge with a curved wall in the background. Two other versions of the work exist, one in the Ashmolean Museum, Oxford and another discovered in 1979 in a private collection in France. They have been dated to *c.* 1733 when the artist began to paint his first genre scenes.

Bartolomeo Schedoni
*The Rest on the Flight
into Egypt*
Oil on panel, 30.5 by 39.4 cm
(12 by 15½ in)
New York $772,500
(£471,225) 28.1.99

This painting is typical of
Schedoni's ability to imbue
an oft-depicted subject with
a sense of the human and the
real. The intimacy of the
scene is further heightened
by its scale, the massing of
all the figures on the left, the
diagonal of faces and hands
and especially by both the

supernatural light
illuminating the figures as
well as the moonlight
reflected off the lake.
Bartolomeo Schedoni's
career, which lasted a mere
15 years, was centred on the
courts of the Este in Modena
and the Farnese in Parma,
where the collections of Old

Master and contemporary
paintings no doubt
influenced his style.
However, it was the work
of Correggio that seems to
have provided the most
constant source of
inspiration for the artist.

Giovanni di Niccoló de Luttero, called Dosso Dossi
Venus Awakened by Cupid
Oil on canvas, 120.5 by 157 cm (47½ by 61¾ in)
London £991,500 ($1,556,655)
8.VII.99

Dosso's *Venus Awakened by Cupid* relates stylistically to other works by him from the mid 1520s. The dramatic lighting and sweeping vista, for example, recall his *Apollo musico* now in the Galleria Borghese, Rome. For much of the 17th century the painting formed part of the celebrated Barberini collection, but its subsequent whereabouts are unknown until it was rediscovered in 1980. The survival of a full-scale work by the most famous court painter of Renaissance Ferrara is a great rarity.

Meindert Hobbema
The Castle of Ootmarsum
(Het Huis Ootmarsum)
Signed *m hobbema*
Oil on canvas, 40.6 by
52.4 cm (15½ by 20½ in)
London £1,596,500
($2,682,120) 17.XI.98

Het Huis Ootmarsum has
been dated to the late 1660s
and shows a castle close to
the present Dutch–German
border. The earliest record of
the building is 1273; it was an
outpost of the Teutonic
Knights for about 300 years,
finally being destroyed

between 1818 and 1825. The
painting belonged to the
19th-century philanthropist
Angela Burdett-Coutts and
was sold in 1922 with other
paintings from her
collection, which included
works by Reynolds,
Gainsborough, Rembrandt

and Turner. With another
Hobbema, sold separately,
Het Huis Ootmarsum was
the second most expensive
Old Master in the 1922 sale,
the first, at 7,000 guineas,
being a panel by Raphael.

Hendrick Martenesz. Sorgh
A Musical Company
Signed and dated *1661*
Oil on canvas, 68 by 82 cm
(26¾ by 32¼ in)
London £969,500
($1,628,760) 17.XII.98

It was not until its recent exhibition in 1980 that this painting, hitherto not published or exhibited for nearly 50 years, received recognition as one of Sorgh's finest achievements. This type of subject is in fact relatively rare in Sorgh's oeuvre which, up to 1661 when this was painted, had chiefly consisted of low-life peasant subjects or the kitchen and market scenes for which he is best known.

Nicolaes Berchem
Landscape with Travellers
Signed and dated
N. Berchem 1657
Oil on canvas, 66.7 by
76.2 cm (26¼ by 30 in)
New York $800,000
(£488,000) 28.1.99

A prolific member of what is considered the second generation of Dutch Italianate landscape painters, there is, in fact, no evidence that Berchem visited Italy. However, given the complete absorption of light and atmosphere in his work, there seems little doubt that he travelled there, possibly in the early 1650s, a few years before the present picture was painted. Berchem worked in both Haarlem and Amsterdam, where he produced over 50 etchings and a compellingly large body of drawings and paintings. This piece combines Berchem's typically warm, light handling of paint, rural staffage and impressive flora in a magnificent landscape.

Hendrick Frans van Lint, called Lo Studio

An Extensive Landscape with Venus, Apollo and Cupid, Silenus and Other Classical Figures and Temples (above); *An Extensive Classical Landscape with Figures Paying Homage to Pan* (below)
A pair, signed, inscribed and dated *1742*
Both oil on canvas, in contemporary gilt wood frames, each: 62 by 74.5 cm (24½ by 29¼ in)
London £441,500 ($693,155)
8.VII.99

A native of Antwerp, van Lint moved permanently to Rome in around 1710, where he became a member of a confraternity of Northern painters called the '*schildersbent*'. He earned the nickname 'Lo Studio' due to the painstaking precision with which he rendered figures and architecture in his work and he often signed himself with the name, as here. By the 1730s van Lint had made a reputation painting *vedute* of buildings in and around Rome, and also turned his hand to painting overtly Classical subjects set in landscapes heavily inspired by the works of Claude Lorrain. These two views are among the finest examples of van Lint's 'Claudian' landscapes.

OLD MASTER DRAWINGS

Pieter Coecke van Aelst
The Sacrifice at Lystra
(Acts 14: 13–15)
Inscribed, pen and brown ink
and wash heightened with
white, 29.6 by 46.4 cm
(11⅝ by 18¼ in)
New York $343,500
(£209,535) 27.1.99

This newly discovered
drawing belongs to a highly
important series of designs
executed by van Aelst for
nine tapestries illustrating
scenes from the life of
St Paul. The biblical text
illustrated here relates how
the natives of Lystra, in

thanks for a miracle worked
by St Paul, healing a man
who had never walked, began
to prepare sacrifices to the
deities Mercury and Jupiter.
St Paul and St Barnabas
stopped them and exhorted
them to turn to the worship
of God.

Francesco Maria Mazzola, called Il Parmigianino

Recto and *verso*: composition studies for *La Madonna dal collo lungo*
Red chalk heightened with white, over stylus (recto); pen and brown ink (verso)
19.4 by 13.2 cm (7⅝ by 5¼ in)
London £254,500 ($402,110)
7.VII.99

Parmigianino's famous painting *La Madonna dal collo lungo* was left incomplete due to the artist's insatiable desire for perfection and was only installed in the chapel of Santa Maria de'Servi, Parma, in 1542, two years after his death. The numerous surviving studies for the composition – around 30 – bear witness to the great efforts Parmigianino put into the painting, which epitomizes his highly original style.

Hendrick Goltzius

Rebecca, Wife of Isaac
Pen and brown ink and wash and red chalk, heightened with white
20.8 by 16.1 cm (8⅛ by 6⅜ in)
London £342,500 ($541,150)
7.VII.99

Recently rediscovered, this is a preparatory study for the second print in the series of three representations of the *Wives of the Patriarchs*. The other two compositions in the series are *Leah and Rachel, Wives of Jacob*, now in the Brussels Museum, and *Sarah, Wife of Abraham*. Hendrick Goltzius (1558–1617) was at the peak of his powers as a draughtsman at the time of this work, around 1597; in this remarkable drawing he has produced not only a carefully executed design for a print, but also, with its sophisticated working up in red and white, an exquisite, finished work of art.

George Stubbs, ARA
Baron de Roebeck Riding a Bay Hunter
Signed *Geo. Stubbs pinxit 1791*
Oil on canvas, 101.5 by 127 cm (40 by 50 in)
London £2,091,500 ($3,346,400) 8.VI.99

This painting, of Swedish nobleman John, 2nd Baron de Roebeck, was completed in 1791, a year in which the artist's fortunes seemed to have greatly improved since the disappointments of the previous decade. It was the year that saw the beginning of substantial patronage of Stubbs by George, Prince of Wales. Among the pictures painted for the Prince in that year were the equestrian portrait of the Prince by the Serpentine, *John Gascoigne with a Bay Horse* and *Baronet with Samuel Chifney Up*. This painting was unknown until it appeared at the Stubbs exhibition at the Walker Art Gallery in 1951. It later appeared for auction at Sotheby's in 1960 where it was sold by a direct descendant of the Baron.

Johann Zoffany, RA

Portrait of Henry Knight of Tythegston (1738–72), with His Three Children, Henry (1763–1825), Robert and Ethelreda

Oil on canvas, 236 by 146 cm (93 by 57½ in)

London £1,101,500 ($1,762,400) 8.VI.99

This portrait was commissioned by Henry Knight of Tythegston in Glamorganshire in 1770. By this time Zoffany, originally from Germany, had lived in London for ten years and had established himself as the undisputed master of the conversation piece. In 1770 he exhibited for the first time at the Royal Academy, having been nominated a member by George III, and was busy working on several large-scale portraits of various members of the Royal Family. It is not clear how Knight came to commission the painting, but it may simply be that he wished to commission the most fashionable artist of the time. The portrait is a fine example of Zoffany's ability to arrange groups and shows a lightness and spontaneity of approach. This painting was purchased by the National Gallery of Wales.

Allan Ramsay
Portrait of a Young Girl, said to be the Artist's Niece
Signed A. Ramsay/1744
Oil on canvas, 97 by 123 cm
(38 by 48½ in)
London £419,500 ($671,200)
8.vi.99

Allan Ramsay painted this enchanting portrait in London following his extended stay in Italy. The natural charm and sophisticated composition of the picture illustrate how much Ramsay had learnt from Imperiali and Batoni in Rome. His new confidence is evinced in the celebrated phrase he wrote to his friend and travelling companion, Alexander Cunyngham: 'I have put all your Vanlois and Soldis and Roscos to flight and now play the first fiddle my Self.' The identity of the sitter has always remained a mystery, from the 19th century the portrait was said to be of the artist's niece but none of Ramsay's sisters married. It seems likely that, following his wife's sudden and tragic death, Ramsay became close to her family and the girl could well be Anne Ramsay's niece or at least a connection of the family. Ramsay's chalk study for the pose is now in the collection of the National Galleries of Scotland.

BRITISH WATERCOLOURS

Joseph Mallord William Turner, RA
Bedford, Bedfordshire
Watercolour with touches of bodycolour and scratching out and stopping out,
34.9 by 48.9 cm
(13¾ by 19¼ in)
London £331,500 ($530,400)
8.vi.99

This magnificent watercolour was drawn as part of a project undertaken by Turner and the engraver Charles Heath to publish engravings of *Picturesque Views in England and Wales*. Described by Ruskin as 'the great central work of Turner's life', the project was dogged by financial difficulties but the resulting engravings were outstanding and the watercolours, of which Bedford is one of the finest, are recognized as among Turner's most important works. Eric Shanes described them as 'unsurpassed in their range and power'.

Samuel Palmer
The Colosseum, Rome
Watercolour over pencil
heightened with bodycolour
and gum arabic, 27 by 42 cm
(10½ by 16½ in)
London £34,500 ($57,270)
26.XI.98

Dating from Palmer's
honeymoon trip to Italy,
1837–39, this rare work
shows a view of the
Colosseum from the
northeast with the Arch
of Constantine to the right.
In the foreground are old
Roman remains with
pentimenti revealing a cart
and oxen. Like many of
Palmer's Italian works, it is
unfinished and appears to
have been drawn as a record
of the view for later use.
However it shows the artist
at his least self-conscious,
displaying the freedom of
expression and virtuosity
often missing from his
later work.

John Robert Cozens
*Lake Nemi, Looking
Towards Genzano*
Watercolour over pencil,
36 by 52 cm (14¼ by 20½ in)
London £96,100 ($159,526)
26.XI.98

Cozens visited Lake Nemi
during trips to Italy in
1776–79 and 1782–83 and, in
response to demand from
patrons, drew nine
watercolours of the subject.
Several of these bear dates
ranging from 1778 to 1790.
In this previously unrecorded
version of the subject the
artist chose not to paint a
faithful depiction of the lake,
but instead included all the
points of interest in the
surrounding area to create
a single landscape.

VICTORIAN PICTURES

John William Waterhouse, RA, RI
The Awakening of Adonis
Signed and dated 1899
Oil on canvas, 95.9 by 188 cm
(37¾ by 74 in)
New York $2,340,000
(£1,404,000) 10.XI.98

The Awakening of Adonis, which was included in the Royal Academy's Summer Exhibition of 1900, takes its subject from Greek and Roman mythology. Here, Aphrodite awakens the sleeping Adonis with a kiss, while Cupid, accompanied by a band of children holding flowers, blows on a torch to rekindle the flame of desire that burns in the hearts of the two young lovers. The surrounding flowers underline the symbolic nature of the story, which, in the hands of Waterhouse, represents both the eventual demise of Adonis, as red and purple anemones grew from where his blood was shed, and the renewal of life and love at the arrival of spring. Written accounts of the painting when it was first shown dwelt on the delicacy and subtlety of this symbolic treatment. By all critics, Waterhouse was praised as an artist who had learnt from the example of the Old Masters and had a profound knowledge and understanding of his literary subjects.

Sir John Everett Millais, PRA
James Wyatt and his Granddaughter, Mary Wyatt
Signed with monogram *JEM* and dated *1849*
Oil on panel, 35.5 by 45 cm (14 by 17¾ in)
London £661,500 ($1,058,400) 8.VI.99

James Wyatt (1774–1853) was a prominent figure in mid-19th-century Oxford. He was Mayor in 1842–43 and ran a successful print shop which was visited by many young artists including various members of the Pre-Raphaelite Brotherhood and followers of John Ruskin.

Wyatt seems to have met Millais in 1846, which is the date of a watercolour portrait of Mary his granddaughter, the same child as seen here. In 1849, Wyatt acquired one of Millais's early works *Cyman and Iphigenia* and commissioned the picture illustrated here and its

pendant portrait of his daughter-in-law, Eliza, and her daughter, Sarah.

MODERN BRITISH PAINTINGS

Sir Stanley Spencer, RA
The Garage
Oil on canvas, 101.5 by
152.5 cm (40 by 60 in)
London £1,046,500
($1,663,935) 23.VI.99
Sold on the Instructions of
The National Motor
Museum Trust

Spencer painted *The Garage*
at the same time as he was
engaged upon the Sandham
Memorial Chapel at
Burghclere. The
monumental scale of the
picture is an echo of his
majestic aspirations for the
chapel, but it is otherwise a
very different conception:
where the Burghclere series

recalls an elegiac past, *The
Garage* looks forward to a
world of industry and
technology. It represents a
less appreciated side of
Spencer, not as the painter of
Cookham, but much as his
contemporaries must have
conceived him – as a master
of the realist movement in
modern Britain. *The Garage*

was originally conceived as
one of a group of five works
commissioned by the
Empire Marketing Board in
1929, on the theme of
Industry and Peace. Spencer
interpreted this in a highly
personal way, intending to
'give the impression of a
kind of communion of life
and people from a variety of

callings, trades and
professions'. Consequently
The Garage is more than a
workshop scene, it is a
panorama of motoring as
both a technological and a
social phenomenon, and a
milestone in Spencer's
development as a leading
modernist of his time.

David Bomberg
San Miguel, Toledo, Afternoon
Signed and dated 29
Oil on canvas, 71 by 70.5 cm
(28 by 27¾ in)
London £161,000
($268,870) 3.xii.98
From the Hiscox Collection

The monumental Toledo series produced by Bomberg in the autumn of 1929 established him for the first time in his career as a fully mature artist, possessed of a unique and powerful identity of his own. In this work the rigorous structuralism of Bomberg's pre-war abstraction is allied with a new and unfettered relish of colour and the plastic possibilities of paint. Bomberg arrived in the city in September 1929, attracted by the 'romance' of a place unchanged since the time of El Greco. His instinctive response to the hill town was best expressed immediately in paint: intricacy and gusto are combined in a peculiarly intimate evocation of the actual weight and mass of the land itself.

Roderic O'Conor, RHA
Nature morte aux pommes
Oil on canvas, 55.5 by 38 cm
(21¾ by 15 in)
London £276,500 ($461,755)
3.xii.98
From the Hiscox Collection

Painted in the Breton town of Pont-Aven in 1894, *Nature morte aux pommes* is one of the pictures that form the foundation of O'Conor's growing reputation as a central figure in Post-Impressionist painting. Marking the year of his first meeting with Gauguin, it is witness to their friendship and to the influence on both of the work of Cézanne. Most importantly, though, the picture shows dramatically how in this company the Irish artist nonetheless forged a unique and powerful style entirely his own.

Léon-Augustin Lhermitte
En moisson
Signed and dated *1913*
Oil on canvas, 188.5 by
259 cm (74¼ by 102 in)
London £243,500 ($387,165)
28.VI.99

First exhibited to great
acclaim at the Paris Salon of
1913, *En moisson* marks the
zenith of Lhermitte's
exploration of a subject –
labourers harvesting – of
which he had become the
undisputed master. His
elevation of rural subject
matter to a greater level of
meaning was inspired by the
canvases of earlier
champions of the French
landscape tradition,
including Jean-François
Millet, Jules Breton and
Jules Bastien-Lepage. It is
to Gustave Courbet that
En moisson is most indebted;
its oversize canvas and
realistic images of labourers
from Lhermitte's native
village of Mont-Saint-Père
near Rheims all mirror
Courbet's work.

James Jacques Joseph Tissot
Young Ladies Admiring Japanese Objects
Signed and dated 1869
Oil on canvas, 55.9 by 39.4 cm (22 by 15½ in)
New York $2,312,500
(£1,433,750) 5.v.99

By the mid 1860s, Tissot's style had changed from historical subjects to those depicting contemporary life. The resulting works, particularly those of informally posed young ladies in fashionable dress set within elegant surroundings, met with immediate critical acclaim. This occurred at the same time as Tissot was developing a passion for Japanese art, which is clearly expressed in this painting. The composition reveals the artist's brilliance at rendering the human form, as well as at painting intricate still lifes and reproducing the tactile qualities of different surfaces and materials. It is also a clever and engaging comment on the act of looking, as we gaze into a room where young ladies stare dreamily into a glass display case, behind which a garden can be seen, refracted through the panes of a leaded glass window. To the left, we see a Japanese screen, on which there are painted partial views of a scroll painting and a *soji* screen, and behind the screen another leaded window, which seems to reflect the door of the room Tissot has depicted.

William Adolphe Bouguereau
Alma Parens
Signed and dated *1883*
Oil on canvas, 230.5 by
139.7 cm (90¾ by 55 in)
New York $2,642,500
(£1,585,500) 10.XI.98
Property from the Collection
of Sylvester Stallone

When exhibited in the Salon of 1883, Bouguereau's monumental painting, *Alma Parens* created a sensation in the French press. The artist's majestic, allegorical composition depicts a youthful and idealized woman in a noble and hieratic pose, who offers the nourishment of her breast to the children crowding around her. Although the painting might first be taken to symbolize Charity, Bouguereau's remarkable composition presents the viewer with an allegory of France, his motherland, using elements inspired by and borrowed from his numerous compositions of Charity or the Holy Family. The young woman, a truly modern icon, wears a wreath fashioned from ears of corn decorated with flowers in the colours of France. French agricultural produce, such as wheat, apples and grapes, can be found strewn about her feet. Bouguereau's patriotism undoubtedly reflected the growing prosperity of France, which had recovered from the devastating effects of the Franco-Prussian War some 12 years before.

Harald Sohlberg
Oslo fra Akershus
Signed and dated *1933*
Oil on canvas, 94 by 125 cm
(37 by 49¼ in)
London £535,000 ($850,650)
28.VI.99

Oslo fra Akershus depicts
Oslo fjord on a summer
evening from the
Commanding Officer's
Garden at Akershus.
Sohlberg began the serene
composition in 1924 but
would not declare it
complete until 1935, two

years after signing the
canvas. Johan Throne-Holst,
who commissioned the
painting and supported
Sohlberg throughout its long
gestation, remained a firm
friend of the artist until his
death. Sohlberg played a key
role in introducing

stemningsmaleri ('mood
painting'), so typical of
fin-de-siècle Nordic art, to
Norway during the 1890s.
His work is characterized by
an intense and often brilliant
theatricality.

Ferdinand Hodler
Lake Silvaplana
Signed and dated *Sept. 1907*
Oil on canvas, 60 by 90 cm
(23⅝ by 35⅜ in)
Zurich SF4,182,400
(£1,798,432; $2,967,412)
2.XII.98

Ferdinand Hodler is one of many artists and writers to have contributed to the fame of Switzerland's Oberengadin area: others include Hermann Hesse, Alberto Giacometti and Friedrich Nietzsche. Hodler spent ten days there in 1907, staying in the Palace Hotel, St Moritz, and during that time painted eight works. When he saw Lake Silvaplana he commented to Willy F. Burger, a painter friend: 'Once I saw this lake and this unique line, I was decided. It is unique, this lake, the mirror that reflects everything – a response to all the forms that are essential for this composition.' While this painting, Hodler's only landscape from this time to be precisely dated, is almost identical to another in the Zurich Kunsthaus, it has a greater freshness, the wider canvas enabling the artist to capture the calmness of the valley more effectively. *Lake Silvaplana* achieved a world record price for a work by Hodler.

AMERICAN PAINTINGS

Frederic Edwin Church
To The Memory of Cole
Signed *F.E. Church* and
dated *April 1848*
Oil on canvas, 81.3 by
124.5 cm (32 by 49 in)
New York $4,732,500
(£2,981,475) 27.v.99

Church's magnificent
memorial to Thomas Cole,
his teacher and mentor, was
rediscovered in 1980 when
Professor J. Gray Sweeney
identified a painting entitled
Sunrise in the Catskills,
belonging to the Des Moines
Women's Club, as this

important lost work. The
painting had originally been
owned by George W. Austen,
a New York auctioneer and
treasurer of the American
Art-Union, who also owned
Cole's *The Cross In the
Wilderness.* Painted in the
April of 1848, it pre-dates by

almost a year Asher B.
Durand's monumental
Kindred Spirits, which has
long been regarded as the
only work to commemorate
Cole's untimely death in the
winter of 1848. From
Church's painted epitaph to
his beloved master emerges

a profound and complex
work in which the younger
artist pays tribute to Cole's
grand iconographic tradition,
proclaiming himself the
leader of a new style of
American landscape painting.

Martin Johnson Heade
Two Orchids in a Mountain Landscape
Signed *M.J. Heade*
Oil on canvas, 43.2 by 58.4 cm (17 by 23 in)
New York $937,500
(£590,625) 27.v.99

Martin Johnson Heade's beautiful paintings of South American orchids and hummingbirds have long captured the interest of American paintings collectors. This composition's large size, its emphasis on the landscape

in the background and the unusual variety of *Cattleya* orchids most likely indicate that it was painted between 1870 and 1872, when Heade first began exploring the orchid and hummingbird theme. Also included in the composition are a smaller

variety of purple orchids, named *Dendrobium*. The hummingbirds depicted are both male and female gorgeted woodstar, natives of Columbia.

Childe Hassam
July Night
Signed and dated
1898–1900
Oil on canvas, 95.2 by
77.5 cm (37½ by 30½ in)
New York $2,312,500
(£1,387,500) 3.XI.98

July Night was painted in 1898 during the artist's first visit to East Hampton, New York. His friend, and fellow artist, Gaines Ruger Donoho, had invited Hassam and his wife, Maud, to East Hampton for the summer. Maud posed for the present painting in the garden of Donoho's home. Through the use of an unusual palette comprising a variety of iridescent colours, Hassam created an evocative mood that, when combined with his energetic pointillist technique, contributed to the undisputed success of this work. Painted a year after the artist had returned from Europe, where he studied at the peak of the Impressionist movement, *July Night* demonstrates Hassam's strong commitment to American Impressionism.

Frederic Remington
The Belated Traveler
Signed and dated *1906*
Oil on canvas, 50.8 by
66.7 cm (20 by 26¼ in)
New York $2,477,500
(£1,486,500) 3.xi.98

This painting displays a marked departure from the starkly lit, dramatic scenes executed early in Remington's career. Shadowy, mysterious and full of portent, the composition exhibits no obvious

narrative. Instead, Remington allows the viewer to create one for him or herself. The monochromatic palette is accentuated by stars sprinkled across an inky black sky while the moon, which is implied rather than

specifically depicted, acts as a main light source, casting a diffused light over the scene. Remington's contemplative images of night-time, in which the earth and sky are illuminated with soft moonlight and twinkling

stars, account for almost half of the artist's finished compositions during the last decade of his life.

George de Forest Brush
The Picture Writer's Story
Signed *Geo. De F. Brush*
Oil on canvas, 58.4 by
91.4 cm (23 by 36 in)
New York $1,707,500
(£1,024,500) 3.XI.98

This work is one of the most beautiful examples of the artist's representation of tribal culture, its customs, philosophies and rituals. Often described as the poet of America's Indian painters, Brush's first-hand experience of life with the Shoshone and Arapahoe in Wyoming and

the Crow in Montana gave him unique insight into the traditions of the Indian tribes. The composition reveals the interior of a lodge and a brave from the Mandan tribe who tells a tale through pictures drawn upon an animal skin. The influence of Jean-Léon Gérôme,

Brush's mentor, is apparent in the highly finished technique, achieved through layering glazes, as well as his choice of exotic subject matter.

Mary Cassatt
Children Playing with a Cat
1908, signed *Mary Cassatt*
Oil on canvas, 81.3 by
100.3 cm (32 by 39½ in)
New York $2,972,500
(£1,783,500) 3.xi.98

The characteristic warmth
and tenderness found in
Mary Cassatt's most
successful maternal
paintings is evidenced in this
striking composition that
includes a mother with two
children. As is typical of the
mothers and children
Cassatt painted during her

career, each figure is
individually engaged.
Avoiding any note of
sentimentality, Cassatt
renders the figures in a
natural and realistic manner.
Other highly successful
aspects of the work are the
detailed depiction of the
elaborate clothing her

subjects wear, as well as the
focus on colour that
demonstrates a new
direction for the artist. The
combination of the work's
charming intimacy, large
scale and complexity of
composition place it among
Cassatt's most important
works of the 1900s.

LATIN AMERICAN ART

Diego Rivera
Niña con rebozo
Signed and dated 38
Oil on canvas, 82 by 64 cm
(32¼ by 25¼ in)
New York $937,500
(£581,250) 3.VI.99

Diego Rivera lived and
worked in Europe between
1908–21. Upon his return to
Mexico in 1921, he
abandoned Cubism and
European Modernism, which
he had explored in Europe.
Rivera soon became
preoccupied with Mexico's
indigenous cultures and folk
art traditions, which proved
to be a continuous source of
inspiration for him. Painted
in 1938, at the pinnacle of
Rivera's career, this work is
not only a celebration of the
rich cultural heritage of
Mexico but is an excellent
example of Rivera's ability to
masterfully depict a poignant
and timeless subject.

Francisco Narváez
Eva
Limestone, 38 by 123.2 by
21.6 cm (15 by 48½ by 8½ in)
New York $266,500
(£159,900) 23.XI.98

Narváez was born in 1905 in
Venezuela. At the age of 14,
he began his formal art
education in Caracas at the
Escuela de Artes Plásticas
where, years later, he would
be appointed director. He
also attended the Academie
Julian in Paris where he was
exposed to the influence of
Aristide Maillol and the

French Art Deco school. In
his own work, Narváez
transformed the neo-
classical spirit of the
European school into a
new world of Creole
reminiscences. During the
1930s, his sensuous male
and female sculptures were
often turned into fountains
or used to decorate buildings

in Caracas. Narváez's use of
the warm *Cumarebo*
limestone, as in this
masterpiece created in 1940,
as well as tropical
hardwoods, reveals his
desire to work with local
materials, which in turn gives
his work an autochthonous
identity.

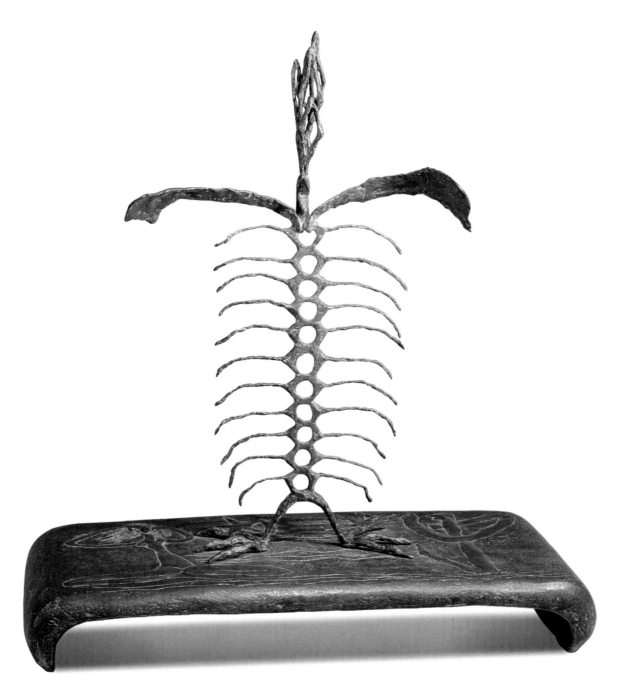

Maria Martins
Brouillard noir (Black Fog)
Signed
Bronze with brownish-green
patina, 88.3 by 76.2 by
36.8 cm (34¾ by 30 by
14½ in)
New York $233,500
(£144,770) 3.VI.99

Born in Brazil, Maria Martins
(1894–1973) began her
career as a concert pianist,
later turning to sculpture,
drawing and painting. Her
marriage to a Brazilian
diplomat meant that she
travelled extensively. She
studied with Oscar Jespers in
Brussels in 1939 and in 1941
had her first exhibit at the
Corcoran Gallery in
Washington, DC. In the
1940s she exhibited in New
York and Brussels, and her
first exhibition in Brazil was
at the Museu de Arte
Moderna de São Paulo in
1950. Today her work can be
seen in museum collections
in Brazil, the United States,
France and Argentina.
Brouillard noir was executed
in 1949.

Mario Carreño
La diosa del mar
Signed and dated 43
Duco on masonite with
painted seashells, sea fan
and cloth, 94.6 by 118 cm
(37¼ by 46½ in)
New York $321,500
(£192,900) 23.XI.98

Mario Carreño returned to
Cuba in 1942 after studying
in Europe and travelling to
New York. He was consumed
by a renewed interest in the
island's topography; the lush
tropics of the Caribbean
made him approach his work
with new enthusiasm. Duco

was a means for Carreño to
work rapidly with immediate
results, capturing the ever-
changing landscape, with its
brilliant light and colour. In
José Gomez Sicre's
monograph on the artist, he
explains that in 1943 Carreño
took David Alfaro Siqueiros's

use of artificial pigments one
step further by introducing
the element of collage to his
duco paintings. Carreño
applied cloth, shells and
rope, overlaid with duco, to
further enhance the three-
dimensionality of his
compositions.

Pierre-August Renoir
Mademoiselle Grimprel au ruban bleu
Signed and dated 80
Oil on canvas, 41.3 by 31.8 cm (16¼ by 12½ in)
New York $5,392,500 (£3,235,500) 16.XI.98

Following his pivotal 1876 exhibition and the Third Impressionist Exhibition in 1877, Renoir received great critical acclaim for his portraits, leading to an increased number of commissions. Yvonne Grimprel, the sitter in this portrait, was the five-year-old granddaughter of Armand Grimprel, the business partner of Renoir's friend Paul Bérard. Grimprel commissioned portraits of his three grandchildren while Renoir was staying with Bérard at his château in Wargemont, Normandy in the summer of 1880. The portrait, which was shown at the 1882 Salon, was painted at the culmination of Renoir's pure Impressionist phase, and shows a freshness that abated in subsequent years, following his decision to study Classical and Renaissance art.

Berthe Morisot
Cache-cache
1873, signed
Oil on canvas, 46.3 by
55.2 cm (18¼ by 21¾ in)
New York $3,852,500
(£2,350,025) 10.V.99
From the Collection of Mr
and Mrs John Hay Whitney

This work was included in
the landmark first
Impressionist group show of
1874 organized by the avant-
garde as an alternative to the
officially sanctioned
exhibition at the Salon. It was
lent by Edouard Manet, the
leader of the modern

movement and brother-in-
law of the artist. As such, it
reflects Manet's particular
taste and his influence upon
Morisot's stylistic
development. The relatively
restricted palette and open,
flickering brushwork are
reminiscent of Manet's

paintings of the late 1860s
and early 1870s. At the time
of the exhibition, Morisot
received high praise for the
painting's fine artistic feeling
as well as for her graceful
handling of the subject. The
figures depicted are Berthe
Morisot's sister, Edma

Pontillon, and Edma's
daughter Jeanne, who are
playing hide-and-seek in the
landscape surrounding
Edma's father-in-law's
country estate in the village
of Maurecourt, a short
distance from Paris.

Paul Cézanne
L'Estaque vu à travers les pins
c. 1882–83
Oil on canvas, 73 by 92.4 cm
(28¾ by 36⅜ in)
New York $11,002,500
(£6,601,500) 16.XI.98
From the Reader's Digest
Collection

The years 1882 and 1883 were critical in the development of Cézanne's art. The paintings executed by him during that time were to have a profound impact upon the development of 20th-century painting, as is abundantly evident in such extraordinary works as *L'Estaque vu à travers les pins*. During the early 1880s, Cézanne worked frequently at L'Estaque, where he executed this work. The new visual language he developed during those years, epitomized by this composition, presupposes a fundamental difference between painting and reality in nature. The Mediterranean sun in L'Estaque inspired Cézanne thoroughly to investigate the mechanics of his compositions, more so than any of his contemporaries. Moved by a passionate desire to create a new classical syntax while using the vocabulary of Impressionism, he minimized the modelling of trees and houses while still providing them with a gentle and precise relief. In doing so, Cézanne created space and depth in the painting that owe very little to conventional methods of rendering perspective and spatial structure but clearly relate to the interest of the art of the next century.

Claude Monet
Meule
Signed and dated 91
Oil on canvas, 73 by 92 cm
(28¾ by 36¼ in)
New York $11,992,500
(£7,315,425) 11.v.99

Between 1888 and 1891,
Monet executed more than
30 grainstack (haystack)
paintings. The grainstacks

were in a field near his home
in Giverny and were, at his
request, left in the field year-
round so that he could paint
them in every season in
order to observe their
existence in the ever-
changing weather and light.
The complexity and
emphasis upon abstract
elements found in the
grainstack paintings identify

them as a turning point in
the rise of abstract imagery
and underscore them as
harbingers of 20th-century
art. They are among the most
important works executed by
Monet that pre-date his first
series of *Water Lilies*, marking
their creation as a defining
moment in the history of
modern art.

OPPOSITE

Pablo Picasso
Femme nue
c. 1909
Oil on canvas, 90 by 71.5 cm
(35 by 28⅛ in)
New York $11,002,500
(£6,601,500) 17.XI.98
From the Morton G.
Neumann Family Collection

Picasso painted *Femme nue*
at Horta de Ebro, Spain, in
the summer of 1909. The
work of Cézanne profoundly
influenced his first paintings
in Horta, especially with
regard to the emphasis that
he placed on the
interpretation of form as
facet and plane. Picasso's
skillful elisions of near and
distant space and the
character of his brushwork
are also indebted to
Cézanne's pictorial
language. During the
summer months of 1909,
Picasso was preoccupied
with his mistress, Fernande
Olivier, who was in poor
health, suffering from kidney
stones. In a series of
portraits based on her
features, he chose not to
pursue a psychological
approach to her suffering.
Instead, he looked for
analogies between the
shapes and forms of her
body and those of the
mountainous landscape. In
Femme nue, Fernande exists
as a 'motif' from which
Picasso improvises the
reconstruction of geometric,
fragmented shapes.
Moreover, he relates the
crags of the Santa Barbara
mountains to her by covering
her in a cascade of draperies
that echo the rhythms and
shapes of the mountains.
As a result, Picasso produces
a fully integrated image that
is his first fully defined
statement of Analytic
Cubism.

Gino Severini
Danseuse
Signed
Oil on canvas, 61 by 50 cm
(24 by 19⅝ in)
London £1,156,500
($1,827,270) 28.VI.99

Influenced by the
atmosphere of Paris before
the First World War, Severini
combined a new approach to
colour with geometric
rhythms to convey the
sensations of the city. The
woman depicted in this oil of
1913 is probably one of the
dancers from the *café
concerts*, for whom the artist
developed a passion.
Severini moved to Paris in
1906, inspired by his teacher
Giacomo Balla's discussion
of the latest developments in
French avant-garde. Italian
Divisionism, celebrated in
the *Manifesto of Futurist
Painters* of which Severini
was a signatory in 1910,
sprang from the same
interest in optics and the
physics of light that was
to inform the Neo-
Impressionism of Seurat.
Severini, having little
knowledge of this
movement, was immediately
captivated by the work of
Signac and Seurat.

Pablo Picasso

Nature morte à la bouteille de rhum
Signed and dated 1914
Oil and sand on canvas laid down on masonite, 38.1 by 46.3 cm (15 by 18¼ in)
New York $7,922,500 (£4,832,725) 10.V.99
From the Collection of Mr and Mrs John Hay Whitney

Picasso moved to Avignon with Eva Gouel whom he had first met in November 1911, in June 1914. The year 1914, between Analytical and Synthetic Cubism, has been described as 'an effervescent year in Picasso's work. He was never more inventive, more cheerful, more delighted with color and pattern, more curious about the small things and happier animating them in his work' (Jean Sutherland Boggs, *Picasso and Things*, exhibition catalogue, Cleveland Museum of Art, 1992, p.132). It should be noted, however, that Picasso held the present work in high esteem, 'When the artist put his retrospective together in Paris in 1932, the only exhibition he is supposed to have selected himself, he took this work sufficiently seriously to have borrowed it from Gertrude Stein' (Boggs, p.164).

Wassily Kandinsky

Ohne Titel (Aquarelle mouvementée)
Signed with the monogram and dated *23*, inscribed *No. 109 Aquarelle mouvementée* and dated *1923*
Watercolour and pen and ink on paper, 33 by 47.5 cm
(13 by 18¾ in)
London £826,500
($1,305,870) 28.vi.99

Wassily Kandinsky's (1866–1944) arrival in Weimar in June 1922 to take up a teaching position at the Bauhaus coincided with the moment in the school's history when it was graduating from the expressionism of the early years toward a stricter functionalism and a greater interest in technology. It was

during his years at the Bauhaus that Kandinsky was able to develop and refine his own language of line and colour; in the complex composition illustrated here two small yellow circles pin the richness of incident into place. One, toward the top right of the painting, is outlined in black and bisected by a long black line

bearing great similarities to the lances carried by the horsemen common to Kandinsky's paintings around 1913. The other circle, just off centre, stands out against a less defined circle of white creating a subtle configuration of geometric elements in the contrast between the circle and its border.

Henri Matisse
Robe jaune et robe arlequin (Nézy et Lydia)
Signed and dated 40
Oil and pencil on canvas,
46.5 by 55.5 cm (18¼ by 21¾ in)
London £7,151,500
($11,299,370) 28.VI.99

The model wearing the patterned dress in this painting is Matisse's muse, Lydia Delectorskaya, who was hired in 1932 at the age of 22 to care for Madame Matisse. Lydia began to pose for Matisse in 1935, and in 1939 accompanied him to Nice, where they made their home in the Hôtel Régina. While living there Matisse painted a series of works depicting female figures in interior settings, using the bold and decorative style he had favoured since 1938. At the age of 70, having largely turned his back on the outside world, Matisse concentrated almost exclusively on capturing the interior of his rooms in the hotel, constantly rearranging the furniture and other objects, and enlivening the compositions with models. Adrien Maeght described his first meeting with Lydia: 'She was the most beautiful woman I had ever seen. I was dazzled the first time I saw her. She was an admirable woman with a strong character and ended up devoting her life to the artist.'

René Magritte
L'empire des lumières
Signed
Oil on canvas, 50 by 73 cm
(19¾ by 28¾ in)
London £2,311,500
($3,652,170) 28.VI.99

Between 1949 and the mid 1960s Magritte made 26 variations on this particularly compelling subject, of which the present work is not only the final one in oil, but the only one in which a figure plays a prominent part in the composition. It was painted in 1964 or 1965 and contains a number of familiar themes from Magritte's work, such as the bowler-hatted man, the sky and the reconciliation of opposites. Magritte told a friend: 'After I had painted *L'empire des lumières* I got the idea that night and day exist together, that they are one. This is reasonable, or the very least it's in keeping with our knowledge: in the world, night always exists at the same time as day.' In the last decade of his career Magritte expanded on one of his favourite images, the sky, telling a reporter: 'The sky is a form of curtain because it hides something from us. We are surrounded by curtains.' The painting, whose title was chosen by Magritte's fellow Surrealist Paul Nougé, appears unthreatening, yet it challenges the natural order of things and may even be one of the most deliberate Surrealist statements of his late years.

CONTEMPORARY ART

Gerhard Richter
Domplatz, Mailand
Oil on canvas, 275 by 290 cm
(108 by 114 in)
London £2,201,500
($3,632,475) 9.XI.98
Property of Siemens AG

Richter's 1968 painting of the Piazza del Duomo in Milan takes a snapshot as its starting point and inspiration. Richter then deliberately blurs and distorts the image using only two colours, Titanium White and Ivory Black. Each brushstroke is gently feathered into the next, creating a luxurious, rippled surface. Richter has said that he wants to make a photograph out of paint, and commented in 1988 that he attempts 'to retain the anonymous gloss of the photograph, to replace the craftsmanly-artistic with the technical'. This is one of the most significant and influential works from the artist's photo-paintings series, its size, technical brilliance and compositional elegance making it a unique masterpiece. *Domplatz, Mailand* set a new world auction record for the artist.

Brice Marden

Yellows

Signed, titled and dated *1972*
on the reverse of each panel
Oil and wax on linen, in three
parts, 182.9 by 182.9 cm
(72 by 72 in)
New York $1,487,500
(£892,500) 17.XI.98

Yellows is a masterful
example of Marden's colour
panel paintings, in which he
broke away from the all-grey
tones of his early work. At the
beginning of the 1970s the
New York-born artist began
to visit the Greek island of
Hydra on a regular basis, and
the influence upon him of
the sea and warm
Mediterranean light can be
seen by the introduction of
colours other than grey to his
paintings. As in all of his
panel paintings, each panel
is the approximate size of an
adult human body, here in a
bluish-grey and soft, muted
yellows. As in earlier, single-
panel works, the artist's
process is revealed at the
bottom of the painting,
where a multitude of paint
layers are exposed.

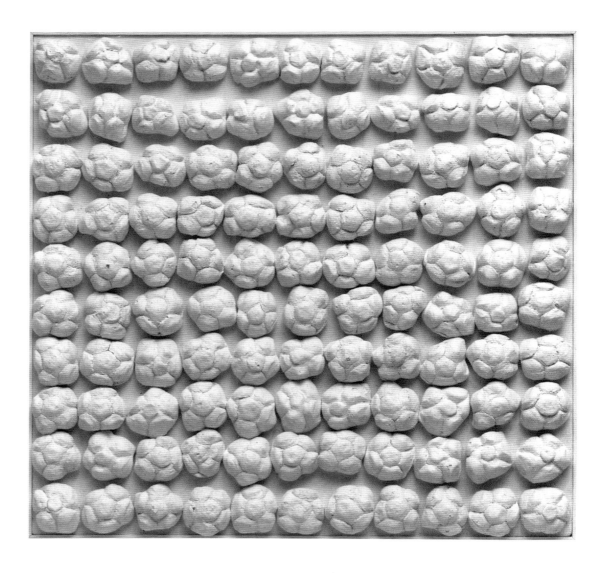

OPPOSITE

Alexander Calder

Constellation
Painted wood and wire,
129.5 by 114.3 by 20.3 cm
(51 by 45 by 8 in)
New York $1,982,500
(£1,229,150) 18.v.99
Property of Theodate and
Scott Severns

Constellation (1943) is one of
about 29 sculptures on this
theme executed by Calder in
the mid 1940s. While Calder
was influenced by Joan
Miró's gouaches and Jean
Arp's sculptural wood reliefs,
his greatest inspiration was
Mondrian, whose studio he
visited in late 1930. His first
wire abstract sculptures were
produced in the years
immediately following this
visit, and it is this form he
returns to for the
Constellations. Calder
described his wire sculptures
in terms of celestial
phenomena: 'The idea of
detached bodies floating in
space, of different sizes and
densities, perhaps of
different colors and
temperatures, and
surrounded and interlaced
with wisps of gaseous
conditions . . . seems to me
the ideal source of form.'

Piero Manzoni

Achrome
Bread rolls and kaolin on
panel, 85 by 90 cm
(33½ by 35½ in)
London £551,500 ($909,975)
9.xi.98

From 1957 Manzoni
produced a series of
Achromes, canvases dipped
in kaolin, some
incorporating other
materials. For this *Achrome*
from 1961–62 he has used
rosette, a typical bread roll
from Milan, to create a three-
dimensional colour vacuum
that throws texture and relief
into the foreground of the
picture plane. By using bread
Manzoni is commenting
upon the sacred nature of the
artist and his media, as well
as the sacred nature of bread
itself in the act of
transubstantiation.
Manzoni's *Achromes*, which
he saw as 'primary spaces',
have been described by
Germano Celant as
exhibiting his interest in
'freezing and immobilizing,
in imprisoning energy'. This
painting achieved a world
auction record for the artist.

Andy Warhol
Marlon
Signed on the reverse
Acrylic and silkscreen ink on
raw canvas, 102.9 by
116.2 cm (40½ by 45¾ in)
New York $2,642,500
(£1,638,350) 18.v.99
Property from the Kraetz
Collection

This is one of approximately
six *Marlon* paintings that
Warhol made by
silkscreening a photographic
still from the 1953 movie *The
Wild One* on to raw canvas.
The choice of Warhol's
subject for this 1966 painting
perhaps indicates his
identification with the
character Brando plays in the

film, who, with his motorcycle
gang, terrorizes a small town.
Brando's clothing was
intended to represent a threat
to 1950s American values, but
by 1966 was considered the
height of fashion by Warhol's
set, all of whom would have
regarded themselves as
outside the conventional
society of their time.

Lucian Freud

Naked Portrait With Reflection
Oil on canvas, 90.3 by
90.3 cm (35½ by 35½ in)
London £2,806,500
($4,630,725) 9.XI.98

While the composition of
this portrait from 1980
recalls the nudes of
Velazquez, its execution is far
from the traditional ideal
nude. Freud reproduces each
feature without sentiment,
using vigorous brushwork to
mould the flesh and
personality of the subject. He
noted in 1987, 'I used to

leave the face until last. I
wanted the expression to be
in the body. The head must
be just another limb.' The
viewer is drawn in by
compositional devices, such
as the strong diagonal thrust
of the couch and figure, and
intellectual ones, particularly
the reflection of Freud's own
feet and legs in the top right-

hand corner of the painting,
which appears to comment
upon presence and absence.
The price achieved by this
painting made it the most
expensive work by a living
artist ever to be sold at
auction in Europe.

OPPOSITE

Andy Warhol
*Campbell's Soup Can
(Chicken With Rice)*
Signed and dated *1962* on
the reverse
Casein and pencil on canvas,
50 by 40 cm (19⅞ by 15¾ in)
New York $1,652,500
(£1,024,550) 18.v.99

*Campbell's Soup Can
(Chicken With Rice)* is an icon
of pop art, its imagery
indelibly impressed in the
public consciousness. Hand
painted with casein rather
than acrylic, and still bearing
the ghostly traces of its
original pencil outline, the
painting is vintage Warhol
at his best, the ideal
testimony to the artist's
extraordinary genius. It was
painted when Warhol was
still experimenting with
different painting processes:
he used hand-made stencils
for the image of the can and
the lettering, and a rubber
stamp for the yellow stars.
Warhol celebrated the solace
of the familiar and canonized
it in his art, explaining the
reason for his choice of
subject: 'I used to drink it. I
used to have the same lunch
every day, for 20 years I
guess, the same thing over
and over again.'

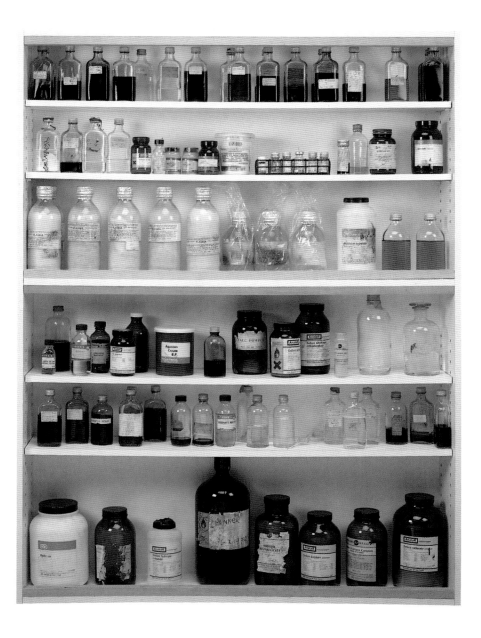

Damien Hirst
My Way
Glass, steel, multi-density
fibreboard, old drug bottles,
137.2 by 101.6 by 22.8 cm
(54 by 40 by 9 in)
London £144,500 ($241,315)
3.xii.98

From the Hiscox Collection
My Way, executed in
1990–91, belongs to a series
of *Medicine Cabinets* that
Hirst began at the end of the
1980s. The title refers to the
Sex Pistols' version of the
song originally made famous
by Frank Sinatra. Hirst's
Medicine Cabinets emerged
from the artist's desire to
question the validity of both
medicine and art, and he
sees the series as embodying
a form that 'everybody could
believe in – I can't
understand why people
believe completely in
medicine and not in art,
without questioning either'.
My Way's simplicity of form
provides immediate visual
appeal, which is
counterbalanced by its
complexity of context. It can
variously be seen as a muse
on mortality, a portrait of
everyman and a self-portrait,
and Hirst has encountered
other interpretations of his
Medicine Cabinets as 'power
structures, a society, or as a
metaphor for the human
body or even as a comment
on capitalism or
consumerism – they are
about all these things'.

PRINTS

Rembrandt Harmensz. van Rijn

St Jerome Reading in an Italian Landscape
Etching and drypoint, on paper with an Arms of Amsterdam watermark with countermark PB (close to Churchill 7, dated 1662)
26 by 21 cm (10¼ by 8¼ in)
London £56,500 ($88,705)
29.VI.99

Rembrandt (1606–69) has always been regarded as the greatest of all exponents of etching and drypoint. He was prolific in his output, producing more than 300 prints mainly composed directly on the copper plate, although there is a preliminary drawing for the present etching. St Jerome compiled the Vulgate, the Latin translation of the Bible, and is usually depicted as an old man in cardinal's dress, with a lion beside him. The buildings in the background reflect Rembrandt's study of Venetian art. Although this print was in the past sometimes described as unfinished, it is in fact a typical and very beautiful example of the artist contrasting highly finished passages with other areas sketched in a free style.

Henri de Toulouse-Lautrec

La clownesse assise (Mademoiselle Cha-u-ka-o)
Lithograph printed in colours, 1896, from the *Elles* series, inscribed in ink by the publisher *Série no 24*, from the edition of 100, published by Gustave Pellet, on fine wove paper, with the watermark *G. Pellet/ T. Lautrec*
Sheet 52.5 by 40.5 cm (20⅝ by 16 in)
London £221,500 ($347,755)
30.VI.99

The series from which this lithograph is taken represents one of the pinnacles of colour lithography. Lautrec regarded the medium as a primary means of artistic expression, and one that afforded him great flexibility. Between 1892 and 1895 Lautrec was a regular visitor to various brothels, sketching and often living with the prostitutes, seeking to portray them without the morality or overt eroticism common in other artists' depictions. In this example Lautrec combines a powerful line and broad planes of colour with original design and a mastery of technique. The price achieved is an auction record for this particular print.

Martin Schongauer
The Wise and Foolish Virgins
Set of ten engravings,
before 1480
Each *c*. 12.2 by 8.6 cm
(4¾ by 3⅜ in)
New York $376,500
(£233,430) 29.IV.99

The text of Matthew 25:1–13 tells of ten virgins awaiting their bridegrooms. Upon the grooms being delayed into the night the Wise Virgins tended their oil lamps, lighting their fiancés' way, but the Foolish Virgins let their lamps go out, missed their grooms' arrival and were unable to marry. In this extremely rare series, of which only 15 complete sets are known to exist, Schongauer demonstrates his ability to illustrate a variety of emotions within a narrow range of expression and pose, with subtle changes to drapery and attitude mirroring the mood of the figure.

Edvard Munch
Madonna
Lithograph printed in colours, 1902, signed in pencil, on thin, soft Japan
Sheet: 64.5 by 48.8 cm
(25⅜ by 19¼ in)
New York $442,500
(£274,350) 30.IV.99

Deeply affected by a series of tragic deaths early in his life, Munch found a release in his art which, he wrote, would depict 'living people who breathe and feel and suffer and love . . . People will understand the sacredness of it, and will take off their hats as though they were in church'. Colour, form and structure all became charged with symbolism which, combined with themes such as death, anxiety and the relationship between the sexes, resulted in a body of work that is intensely expressive.

Claes Oldenburg

Profile Airflow
Cast-polyurethane relief over two-colour lithograph on Special Arjomari paper, mounted on wooden stretcher bars, 1969, signed in pencil, dated, titled and numbered *22/75* on the paper, published by Gemini G.E.L., contained in original aluminium frame
Overall: 85.1 by 166.4 cm (33½ by 65½ in)
New York $43,700 (£27,094)
1.V.99

The preoccupation with scale, material and consumer culture that is seen in Oldenburg's monumental sculptures also informs his printed work. Here, in contrast to his huge three-dimensional versions of everyday objects such as spoons, shuttlecocks and lollipops, a car has been reduced to a transparent relief on grid paper, perhaps suggesting that a prototype is literally taking shape on the drawing board.

Lucian Freud

Kai
Etching printed with tone, 1991–92, initialled in pencil, numbered *10/40*, on Somerset wove paper
69.5 by 54.5 cm (27⅜ by 21½ in)
London £14,950 ($24,368)
24.III.99

Lucian Freud was born in Berlin in 1922, moved to Britain in 1932 and was naturalized in 1939. He studied at the Central School of Art and Goldsmiths' College, and was able to work full time as an artist after being invalided out of the Merchant Navy in 1942. Specializing in portraits and nudes, he prefers to portray people he knows well. His portraits are often intense close-ups, and are sometimes referred to as 'hyperrealist' or 'superrealist'.

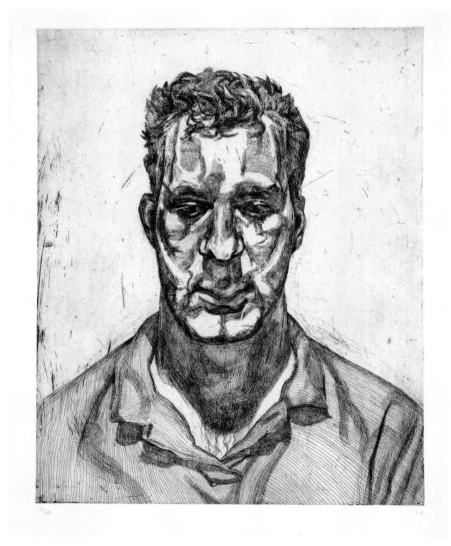

PHOTOGRAPHS

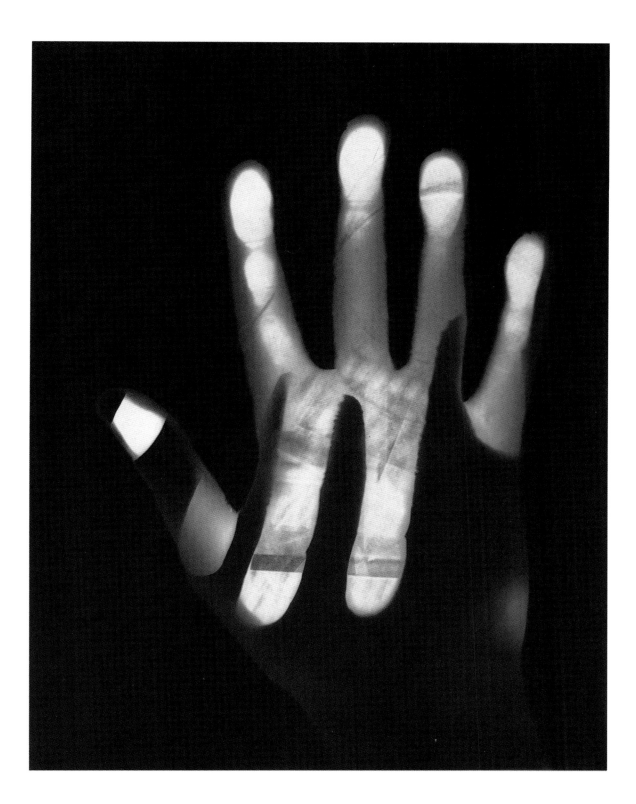

László Moholy-Nagy
Photogram, 1925
Silver print, the reverse
signed, dated and inscribed
in pencil *fotogramm/Moholy-
Nagy/1925*
23.8 by 17.9 cm (9⅜ by 7 in)
London £166,500 ($271,395)
6.v.99

Moholy-Nagy made many
experiments with the
photogram process
throughout the early 1920s,
publishing his first efforts in
1923. The technique of fixing
the play of light and shadow
directly on to photographic
paper, thus eliminating the
need for a camera, fascinated
Moholy-Nagy, who saw the
light-sensitive paper as a
clean sheet upon which he
could compose with light
just as a painter used colour
and canvas. He described
the resulting images created
by this improvised method
as 'vision in motion' and the
'absolute filmic art'. This
unique original experiment
set a world record price for
the photographer.

Charles Sheeler
Abstract – Ford Plant, 1927
Warm-toned, signed, titled
and dated by the
photographer in ink
23.8 by 19.1 cm
(9⅜ by 7½ in)
New York $233,500
(£137,765) 7.x.98

In 1927, painter and
photographer Charles
Sheeler was asked to
produce a series of
documentary photographs
for the Ford Motor Company.
Sheeler concentrated on
Ford's River Rouge plant, at
the time the largest
industrial complex in the
world, which had been
conceived of by Henry Ford
as a self-contained facility
capable of total automobile
production. The massive
utilitarian structures of the
plant provided ample subject
matter for Sheeler, who
believed that the external
evidence of industry served
as a symbol for modern life.
This image of the west side
of the plant's Blast Furnace A
was used as the basis for his
1947 painting *Industrial
Forms* in which the major
structures in the photograph
are present in a simplified,
abstracted form.
Photographs from Sheeler's
River Rouge series rarely
come up at auction. This
example achieved a world
record price for the
photographer at auction.

LITERARY PROPERTY

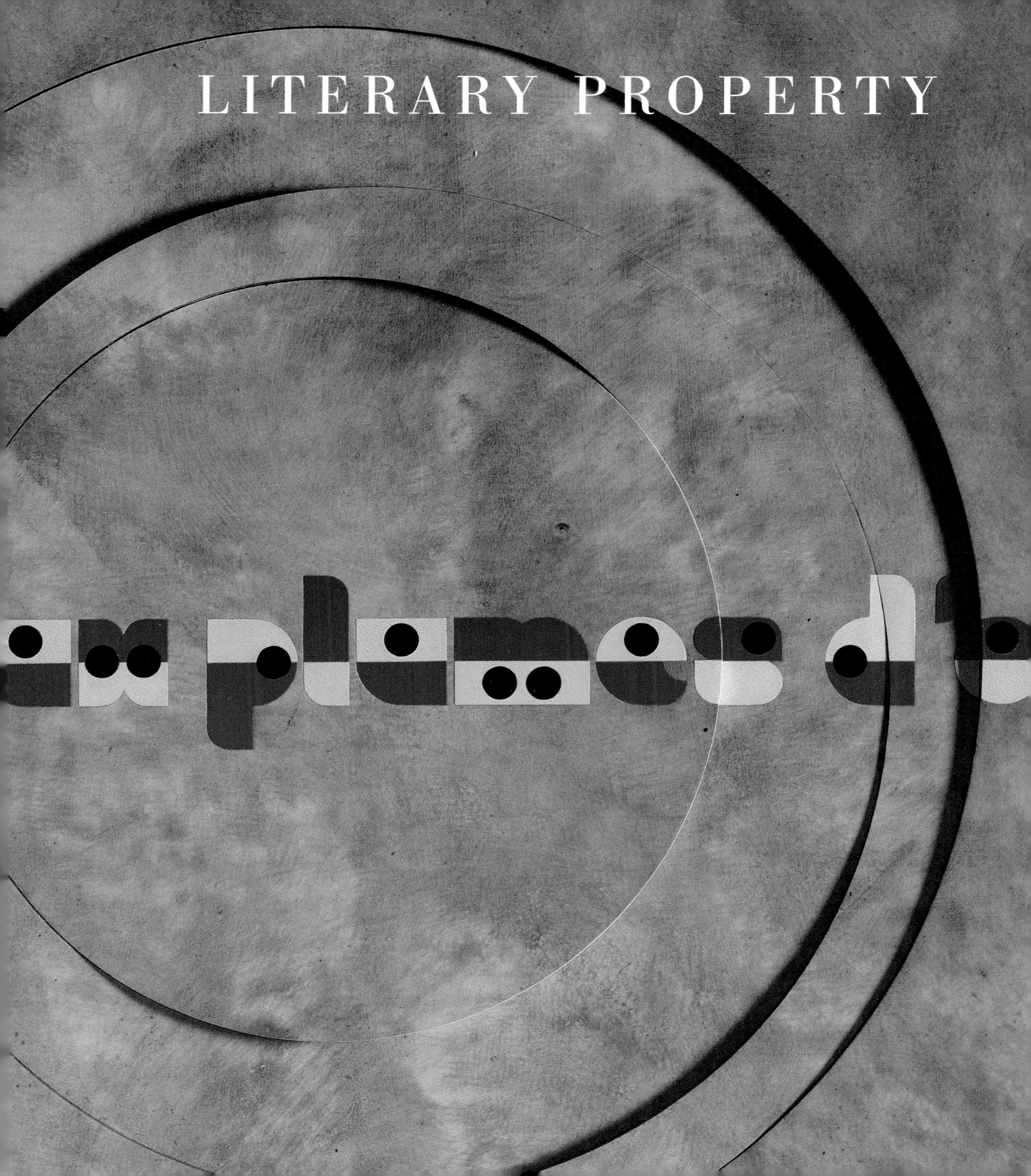

WESTERN MANUSCRIPTS

**The Antiphoner of
San Sisto in Piacenza**

Lombardy, *c.* 1460–80
London £199,500 ($329,175)
1.XII.98

This is a gigantic manuscript choirbook illuminated with 31 very large historiated initials. The whole book is, in fact, the missing volume from an entire set of 14 similar choirbooks preserved in public collections in La Spezia and New York. They were made for the ancient Benedictine abbey of San Sisto in Piacenza, south-east of Milan. The principal artist had also worked on the choirbooks of San Giorgio Maggiore in Venice, and was probably an itinerant professional painter. When the abbey of San Sisto was closed under Napoleon in 1810, its choirbooks passed into private hands and remained together until soon after 1878, when they were finally sold. The present volume remained untraced until it was brought into Sotheby's in Paris in the summer of 1998.

A Figure of a Jew in the Margin of a Single Leaf from the Ghistelles Hours

South-west Flanders, c. 1300
London £19,550 ($32,258)
1.XII.98

The so-called Ghistelles Book of Hours was perhaps made for John III (d. 1315), lord of Ghistelles and Ingelmunster. Many of its borders included little drawings of contemporary figures, from knights to peasants and minstrels. The remarkable feature of the present leaf is that it shows a Jew, wearing the characteristic Jewish hat and frock-coat, and shown with a long beard, book and traveller's staff. Unlike many medieval Christian pictures of Jews, the man is depicted sympathetically. He stands beside a sentence of text from the book of Job, 'Have pity upon me. . . why do you persecute me?' The Jews were expelled from Flanders in 1309.

A Fragment of a Manuscript written in Luxeuil Minuscule

Luxeuil, late 7th or 8th century
London £34,500 ($54,855)
22.VI.99

This is a hitherto unrecorded bifolium (or pair of leaves) from one of the oldest surviving manuscripts written in what is now France. The text is from the encyclopaedic commentary on the book of Job, composed by St Gregory, who died in 604. The present manuscript was copied by the monks of the Irish abbey of Luxeuil in Burgundy, east of Langres, and is written in the famous and strange-looking cursive script known as 'Luxeuil minuscule', characteristic of the abbey's scriptorium. Luxeuil was sacked and destroyed by the Vikings in the early 730s, and its primitive script was never used again. The manuscript of St Gregory had evidently reached England by the early 19th century when a number of its loose leaves were dispersed as curiosities among antiquarians. The main portion of the book is in the British Library, acquired in 1841.

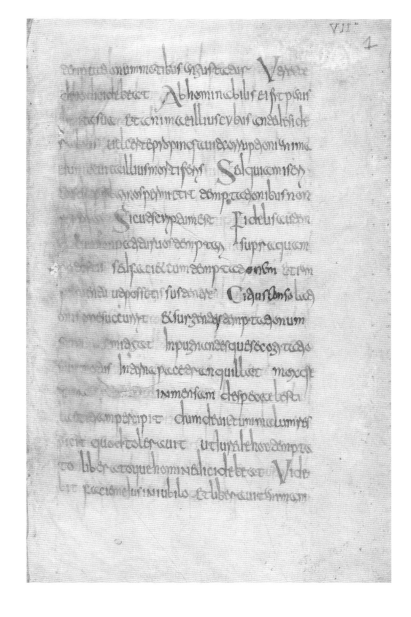

Robert Schumann
Autograph working manuscript of the *Spanisches Liederspiel*, Op. 74, together with two of the *Spanische Liebeslieder*, Op. 138, in their original versions with accompaniment for solo piano
23 pages, folio, 2 songs dated *29 March 1849* and *1 April 1849*
London £122,500 ($203,350)
4.XI.98

The *Spanisches Liederspiel* is one of Schumann's most original and attractive song cycles, arranged for one to four voices. This composing manuscript includes significant differences from the published versions of the songs and has extensive annotations, revisions, deletions, alterations and corrections. It offers insights into the process of composition, in particular the design of the song cycle and the order of the songs, showing that two from Op. 138 were written with those from Op. 74, and, at one point, included in the song cycle.

Johann Sebastian Bach

The first edition of *Die Kunst der Fuge*
Leipzig, 1752
Oblong folio, uncut and unpressed
London £80,700 ($130,734)
21.V.99

This first edition of *The Art of Fugue*, which achieved a world auction record for a piece of printed music, is one of the rarest and most beautiful examples of its kind from the 18th century. Although Bach died in 1750 it seems that he oversaw the publication of this unfinished work, which was probably printed in 1749 and issued later. Only a tiny proportion of Bach's music was published before the 19th century and all these editions are rare: only around 20 copies are recorded. The sharpness and clarity of the printing on this one shows that it must have been one of the earliest impressions.

Claudio Monteverdi

Autograph letter, signed, to a nobleman about the composition of a canzonetta, 23 February 1630
1 page, folio
London £84,000 ($139,440)
4.XII.98

Claudio Monteverdi is a highly influential figure in the history of music, the first great composer of opera and is arguably the greatest composer of the 17th century. This letter is a rare example of the composer's hand, the probable recipient being his patron, Enzo Bentivoglio, Marquis of Gualtieri (1575–1639). Monteverdi thanks his patron for the commission to compose a canzonetta, and apologizes for not having completed it, going on to praise Bentivoglio effusively. All autograph manuscripts of Monteverdi's musical works have apparently been lost and only one other letter is privately owned: the great majority of his surviving correspondence is stored in libraries in Italy.

John Adams, Autograph Signed Letter to Archibald Bulloch, First President of the Provincial Congress of Georgia
3 pages, Philadelphia, 1 July 1776
New York $635,000 (£400,050) 22.vi.99

This letter is extraordinary as it is from one of the signatories to the Declaration of Independence, John Adams, who became the second president of the United States. In it Adams announces the congressional debate surrounding the Declaration: 'This morning is assigned for the greatest debate of all. – A Declaration that these Colonies are free and independent States, has been reported by a Committee appointed some weeks ago for that purpose, and this day, or tomorrow is to determine its fate. – May Heaven prosper, the new born Republic, and make it more glorious than any former Republicks have been.'

John Harrison's 'Journal', documenting all his dealings with the Commissioners for Longitude from 12 March 1761 to 23 May 1766
114 pages, folio
London £89,500 ($150,360) 17.xii.98

The timepieces of John Harrison (1693–1776) are among the most remarkable and original works in the history of technology. He is regarded as the man who solved the greatest scientific problem of his age: how to read longitude accurately at sea. The problem was immense, causing countless disasters at sea due to inaccurate navigation. Parliament offered an immense fortune of up to £20,000 to anyone who could solve it. Harrison after many years produced four balance-controlled sea clocks, vital for measuring longitude precisely. Far from reaping the rewards, however, Harrison faced the massive task of proving to the government that the requirements had been met. This 'journal' represents a record of his efforts. Although Harrison received altogether £23,065 for his work, he was never officially recognized as the winner of the prize.

Robert E. Lee, a Signed Clerical Transcript of General Order No. 9

New York $134,500 (£80,700) 15.XII.98

On the day after Confederate commander Robert E. Lee surrendered to Ulysses Grant at Appomattox Courthouse in 1865 he issued his General Order No. 9, a poignant farewell to the men of the Army of Northern Virginia. Copies were made for transmittal to the army staff and this copy may have been signed by Lee at Appomattox Courthouse. The document is written with great dignity, commending the troops with whom Lee fought: 'With [an] increasing admiration of your constancy and devotion to your country and a grateful remembrance of your kind and generous consideration[s] of [for] myself I bid you [all] an affectionate farewell.' This copy of Lee's valedictory was collected by Archibald Philip Primrose, 5th Earl of Rosebery (Prime Minister 1894–95), who made four visits to the US between 1873 and 1882.

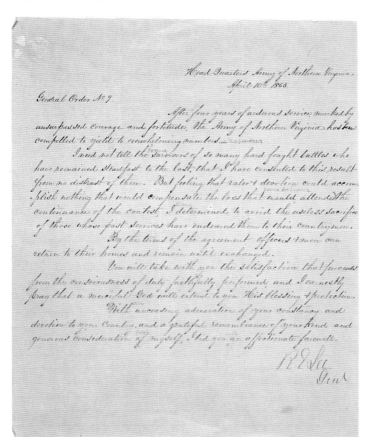

Manuscript Map of Spanish Southwest – Baja Peninsula

entitled *CAMINO DERROTERO QUE CORRE DESDE LAS MISIONES DE S^{AN} DIEGO HASTA SAN XAVIE^R EN VIELA CALIFORNIA*

Signed *Fray Manuel de la Masa, Monterey*, dated in a later hand *1742*

167.6 by 111.8 cm (66 by 44 in)

New York $57,500 (£36,225) 22.VI.99

During the 18th century the Jesuit Order controlled missions and much of the territory in present-day southern California and the Baja Peninsula. Fray Alonso de Carrizo trekked along the route marked on the map in red, visiting ten missions during his journey. He began just south of San Diego, travelling through San Francisco de Borja and Guadalupe to San Xavier. The establishment of missions further south had been prevented by Indian uprisings in the 1730s.

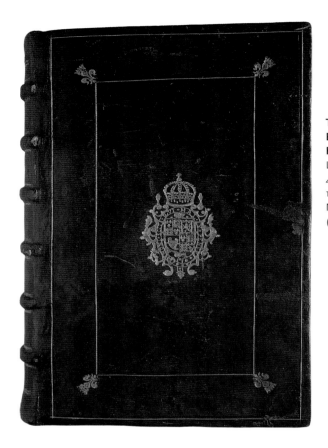

Tall Copy of the First Edition of King James, or Royal, Version of the Bible
London, Robert Barker, 1611
42.2 by 27.6 cm (16⅝ by 10⅞ in)
New York $343,500
(£216,405) 22.VI.99

The King James Bible was royally commissioned in the hope of reconciling, or at least ameliorating, the conflicts between the Bishop's Bible, officially read in services, and the Geneva Bible, more popular among the laity. Two editions of the lectern-size King James Bible were printed close together, they are easily distinguished as the 'He' Bible and the 'She' Bible, according to their readings at Ruth 3:15. The first edition, as here, ends 'and he went into the citie', the second edition reads 'and she went . . .'. The two versions follow the Hebrew and the Latin Vulgate text respectively. Complete and unsophisticated copies in contemporary bindings are increasingly scarce on the market.

A Parisian binding for Jean Grolier of *Councils of the Church*
Brown calf binding, Paris, *c.* 1560
London £144,500 ($229,755) 17.VI.99

The group of ecclesiastical texts, edited by Zaccaria Ferreri, here bound together were all printed in Milan and are concerned with the reform of the Catholic Church. They belonged to the great French collector Jean Grolier, owner of one of the most famous libraries of any period, and famous for the lavishness of the bindings on his books. At the beginning of the 16th century he was in Milan, and was closely interested in the subject matter of these texts. This volume was bound in Paris for Grolier many years later, in the 1540s, towards the end of his life, by the so-called 'Last Binder', and illustrates with its arabesque decoration a new development in style.

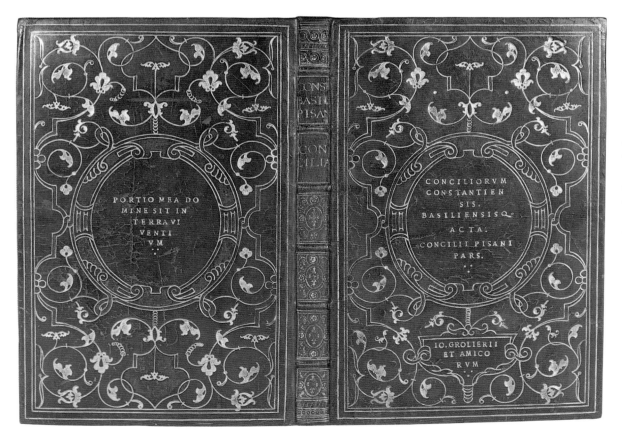

Henry de Ferrières

Livre du roy modus et de la Royne racio

Chambéry: Anthoine Neyret, 1486

London £315,000 ($519,750) 2.XII.98

From the Jaime Ortiz-Patiño Collection

This very rare book, known in some ten copies (of which this is the only one in private hands) is the first printed book on hunting and has 57 delightful woodcut illustrations. The text, attributed to Henry de Ferrières, which is also known in fine manuscript copies, is a dialogue between King Modus and Queen Racio, and was printed by the second printer in Chambéry, a town today chiefly famous for its vermouth, who between 1484 and 1486 produced some six books, all in French.

Giacomo Torelli

Il Bellerofonte

Ten engraved hand-coloured plates, printed on vellum, oblong folio

Venice, 1642

London £177,500 ($282,225) 17.VI.99

These plates, brilliantly coloured by hand by Biagio Lombardo, a miniature painter, and set within an elaborate frame reminiscent of a proscenium arch, form a unique record of stage designs for an opera produced in Venice in 1642. These designs are by the first and greatest stage designer of the Italian Baroque, and are amongst the earliest known for any Venetian opera, the most important dramatic invention of the period. Based on the story of Bellerophon, originally told by Homer in the *Iliad*, the libretto of *Il Bellerofonte* by Vincenzo Nolli survives, although the music by Francesco Sacrati does not. The volume has on its title page the arms of Ferdinand II de Medici, Grand Duke of Tuscany, is bound in red velvet, and may very well have been the copy dedicated and presented to him.

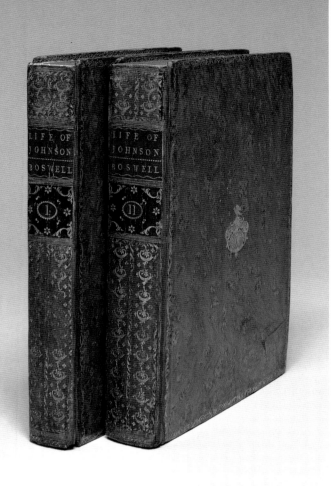

James Boswell

The Life of Samuel Johnson
Two volumes, Henry Baldwin
for Charles Dilly, London,
1793
New York $68,500 (£41,100)
15.XII.98

Inscribed by the author to Dr
John Douglas, Bishop of
Carlisle and later Bishop of
Salisbury, this first edition
presentation copy of
Boswell's great work is
extremely rare. Only three
presentation copies of
Boswell's first book, *An
Account of Corsica*, have ever
come to auction and this is
the first time that a
presentation copy of *The Life
of Samuel Johnson*, the
biography of his celebrated
friend, has ever appeared.
The recipient of these
volumes, Dr Douglas, was a
prolific writer who focused
on exposing fakes, forgeries,
Jansenist miracles and cures
by Royal touch. In this
capacity he assisted Johnson
in dispelling the popular
story of the 'ghost' of Cock
Lane in 1763; Boswell
acknowledges him in the
work, page 22 in volume I,
as 'the detector of great
imposters'.

William Blake

The First Book of Urizen
Lambeth, printed by
Will. Blake, 1794
New York $2,532,500
(£1,570,150) 23.IV.99
Property from the Estate
of Mr and Mrs John Hay
Whitney

One of ten recorded copies
of Blake's mystical retelling
of the Genesis story, the
Whitney copy of *Urizen*, lost
from view for 60 years, set a
new auction record for a
printed work of English
literature. *The First Book of
Urizen* is one of the most
beautiful and challenging of
all of Blake's illuminated
works: written, etched,
printed and coloured by
the artist.

Birds Pl. 54

Tanagra Darwini

Charles Darwin (editor)
The Zoology of the Voyage of H.M.S. Beagle
First complete edition,
5 parts in 3 volumes,
166 plates, Smith, Elder and
Co., London 1840–43
London £38,900 ($66,519)
22.x.98
From the Stanley Smith
Collection of Natural
History Books

This important report on the
zoological collections
obtained by the members of
the Beagle expedition
(1832–36) is rarely found
complete. Darwin
contributed a geological

introduction to Part I (*Fossil
Mammalia*) and a
geographical introduction to
Part II (*Mammalia*), as well
as frequent notes elsewhere.
Part III, *Birds*, has 50 hand-
coloured plates by Elizabeth
Gould, drawn from sketches
by her husband, John Gould,
co-author of Part III. Stanley
Smith was an Australian-born
diplomat and entrepreneur
whose business
achievements allowed him to
pursue his private passions,
many of them connected with
natural history. His collection
of bird books reflected the
many countries in which he
lived, worked or travelled.

Arabella Roupell
*Specimens of the Flora of
South Africa. By a Lady*
London: E. Nicol,
Shakespeare Press, 1849
New York $17,250 (£10,868)
22.vi.99

Arabella Roupell travelled to
the Cape of Good Hope with
her husband between 1843
and 1845. It was there that
she met the famous Danish
physician and botanist

Nathaniel Wallich who
encouraged her to publish
her drawings, which she had
intended strictly 'for the
amusement of leisure
hours'. The book appeared
anonymously in 1849 with
the text by William Henry
Harvey, an expert in South
African botany. This copy was
once the Earl of Derby's,
being one of 103 issued by
subscription only.

Protea mellifera

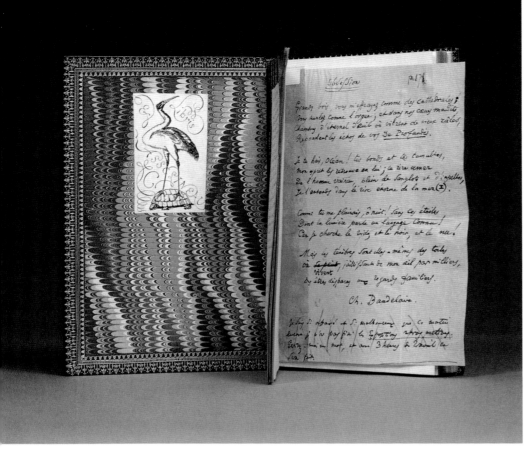

Charles Baudelaire

Les Fleurs du Mal
8vo, Paris: Poulet-Malassis
et de Broise, 1861
London £221,500 ($365,475)
2.XII.98
From the Jaime Ortiz-Patiño
Collection

This is the second edition of
Baudelaire's most famous
work and is enlarged with 35
additional poems. *Les Fleurs
du Mal* first appeared in 1857
whereupon the author was
prosecuted for offences
against public morals (as
was Flaubert for *Madame
Bovary* in the same year).
However, it was the 1861
edition that sealed
Baudelaire's reputation as
one of the greatest poets of
his time. This is one of four
copies printed on the fine
paper called *Chine* in French,
and was given by Baudelaire
to his best friend Charles
Asselineau, who bound an
autograph manuscript of the
poem 'Obsession' at the
front of the volume.

Joan Miró

Le Lézard aux Plumes d'Or
Louis Broder, Paris, 1971
15 lithographs printed in
colours by Miró with binding
by George Leroux
New York $76,750 (£48,352)
22.VI.99

The entire edition of this
book was made up of 195
copies with 20 signed and
numbered by Miró, this
being number 8. Miró's vivid
illustrations to his own text
are perfectly complemented
by Leroux's witty and
beautifully executed binding
of full mottled green calf with
a high lacquer finish. High-
relief geometric ornaments
trimmed in polychrome
calf adorn the binding with
the doublures, the
ornamental linings on the
inside of the book cover,
made of green suede.

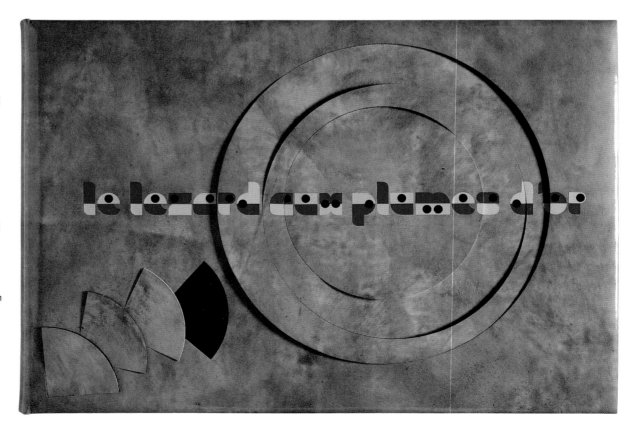

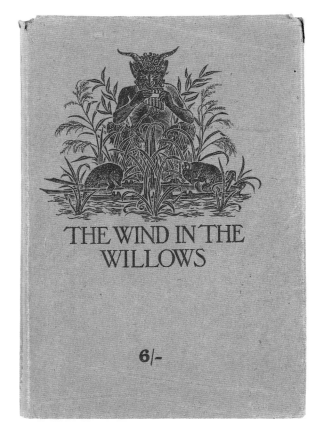
The Wind in the Willows

André Breton

The original autograph manuscript of *Nadja*
25 pages, folio, 9 further pages with letters, photographs and sketches, 1927
London £386,500 ($645,455)
3.XI.98
From the Collection of Henri-Louis Mermod

Nadja is the most famous novel by the so-called 'Pope of Surrealism'. No manuscript of the work was previously known and the appearance of this last December was a major literary event. Given in 1928 by Breton to Mermod, a publisher and collector, whose house in Lausanne was a meeting place for writers, artists and musicians, the manuscript also contains a number of photographs (an art form of particular interest to the Surrealists), viewed by Breton as an integral part of the book, of which none are the same as those that appeared in the first edition of 1928. *Nadja* is semi-autobiographical, and is based on Breton's brief affair with Léona-Camille-Ghislaine D., who called herself Nadja. Breton was fascinated by her unpredictability, and saw in her 'the extreme limit of the Surrealist aspiration', but he soon became bored with her eccentric behaviour, and this manuscript includes some of the letters she wrote to him when he was trying to distance himself from her. He last saw her in February 1927. She was then committed to a psychiatric hospital for the remainder of her life.

Kenneth Grahame

The Wind in the Willows
First edition, with pictorial light-brown dust jacket of the first issue, 8vo, Methuen & Co., 1908
London £44,400 ($73,704)
10.XI.98
The Property of E. E. Bissell

The Wind in the Willows in the first-issue dust jacket is a great rarity amongst children's books, which was reflected in the price, a record for a 20th-century children's book with a dust jacket. Only three other copies have appeared at auction in the last 25 years. Grahame's previous publisher had rejected the book under its preliminary title *The Wind in the Reeds* as it was so different from his earlier work, and Methuen took it on, but refused him an advance, instead agreeing a rising scale of royalties. The book had its earliest beginnings in bedtime stories told to Grahame's son Alastair, over a period of several years.

Henry Moore

18 autograph letters and cards, c.100 pages, 4to and 8vo, 13 September 1926–7 June 1927

London £40,000 ($62,400)
15.VII.99

These letters and cards, some illustrated, were sent to Evelyn Kendall, with whom Moore had an affectionate, but not romantic, relationship. Moore had finished his training at the Royal College of Art and was developing his own sculptures while teaching part-time at the Royal College. Evelyn Kendall had also been a student there, and went on to work as a commercial artist. These letters include some sketches and a full-page ink-and-wash humorous self-portrait and throw much light on his daily working routine and current sculptures. Moore comments freely upon mutual friends, family and personal news, as well as discussing his work in progress. The letters form a major new unpublished biographical source for Henry Moore.

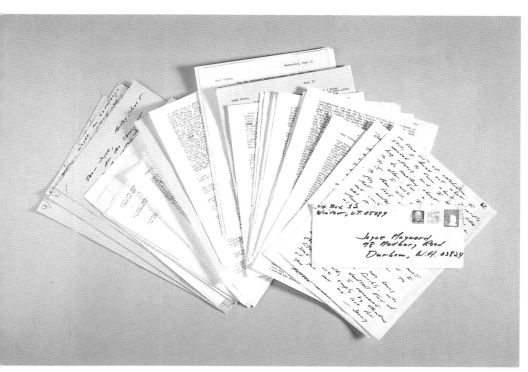

A Series of 14 Letters Written by J. D. Salinger to the Author Joyce Maynard, Dating from 25 April 1972 to 17 August 1973

New York $156,500 (£98,595)
22.VI.99

'One set of letters that make up a crucial piece of my history are the . . . pages of my correspondence with J. D. Salinger . . . Long before I met the author of the letters I fell in love with the voice on the page. Sometimes funny, other moments tender, and frequently wise, knowing and scarily prescient, Jerry Salinger's words formed the basis of my powerful and enduring attachment to him, and haunted me for years after he left my life.' This is how the recipient of these letters, the author Joyce Maynard, described their significance and the power of the nine-month affair – when she was aged 18 and he was 53 – she had with the author of *The Catcher in the Rye*.

ARTS
OF THE
ISLAMIC
WORLD

Portrait of a Lady (perhaps Armenian)
Persia, Isfahan, *c.* 1650–1700
Oil on canvas, framed
163.5 by 90 cm (64¾ by
35¼ in)
London £925,500
($1,573,350) 15.X.98

Setting an auction record
when sold, this magnificent
painting is one of only
12 large Safavid oil portraits
known to exist from this
period. By the mid-17th
century, Isfahan, in northwest Iran, was a major
commercial and cultural
centre. While the unknown
artist was almost certainly
Persian, the area's diverse
influences are reflected not
only in the European style
of the painting, but in the
details of the subject's
clothing, the objects, the
columns behind her and the
distant landscape.

Ibn Sina, Abu Ali al-Husain bin Abd Allah (Avicenna)

Kitab Qanun fi'l-Tibb (The Canon of Medicine), volume 5 (on compound drugs and pharmacopoeia)

Arabic manuscript on paper, Iran or Mesopotamia, dated AH 444 / AD 1052, 82 leaves, 20 lines per page written in clear *naskhi* script in brown ink on buff paper

21.2 by 16.4 cm (8¼ by 6½ in)

London £551,500 ($887,915)

22.IV.99

This manuscript is a remarkably early fragment of perhaps one of the most influential works in the history of medicine. Originating in the early 11th century in western Iran, the Qanun was used throughout the Middle East and Europe as the standard medical textbook for a period of seven centuries. The work was translated into Latin between 1150–87 and a total of 87 translations were subsequently made. It formed the basis of medical teaching at all European universities and appears in the oldest known syllabus of teaching, that of the school of Montpelier in 1309.

A Carved Ivory Box
Islamic Spain, probably
Cordoba, dated AH 394/
AD 1003
36.7 by 7.1 by 4.3 cm (14½ by
2¾ by 1⅝ in)
London £606,500
($1,031,050) 15.x.98

The combination of
decorative elements, and the
dated inscription place this
box within a small surviving
group of ivories carved in
the late 10th and early 11th
centuries under the
patronage of the Islamic
rulers of Spain. The Spanish

Moslem empire at this time
was at its height, and the
works of art produced during
this period reflect the fusion
of Islamic artistic traditions
with those of the indigenous
Jewish and Christian
communities. This box,
created by master craftsmen,

is the only significant
example of dated ivory work
from this period to have
come to auction, the
remainder being in
institutional collections.

**A Gilt-bronze Figure of
Yamantaka**
Imperial China, early Ming
dynasty, late 15th century
Height 80 cm (31½ in)
New York $745,000
(£454,450) 25.111.99

In Tibetan Buddhism
Yamantaka is an emanation
of Manjusri, the god of
wisdom. In this form he
conquered Yama, the demon
king of death. Death in
Tibetan Buddhism is equal to
ignorance; Yamantaka is
therefore saving wisdom
from ignorance, and, despite
his ferocious appearance, is
a compassionate figure. This
Yamantaka, which achieved
a new world record price for
a Himalayan bronze at
auction, is a testament to the
skills of the Imperial Chinese
craftsmen. The figure must
have been commissioned by
the emperor for an important
royal temple, and, despite its
lack of an Imperial reign
mark, can be dated with
confidence on stylistic
grounds to the second half
of the 15th century.

A Nepalese Gilt-bronze Figure of Buddha Sakyamuni
Early Malla period,
*c.*1200–50
Height 50.8 cm (20 in)
New York $508,500
(£305,100) 16.1x.98

The iconography and formal characteristics of Buddha figures such as this example from Nepal can be traced back to as early as the fifth century. The smooth modelling and subtle transitions of the form draped with a transparent garment are features that are remarkably enduring. However, each generation of artists gives fresh variation to this abiding theme. This large gilded Buddha is at once a testimony to a persistent tradition and to a creative vision.

An Illustration to the Ramayana: Rama and Lakshmana Practising their Marksmanship
Mankot, c.1710–20
16.8 by 27 cm (6⅝ by 10⅝ in)
New York $52,900 (£31,740)
16.IX.98

The poem *Ramayana* consists of 24,000 verses in seven books and tells the history of Rama, the seventh incarnation of Vishnu. One episode involves the abduction of Sita, Rama's wife, by Ravana, the demon king, whose name means 'He who makes the world scream'. With the aid of a nation of monkeys, of whom two are shown here, a bridge was built from India to Sri Lanka, Ravana's land. Rama and his invading army gradually overcame the enemy and his arrow slayed the demon.

A Blue and White *Meiping*
Yongle period
36.5 cm (14⅜ in)
Hong Kong HK$11,020,000
(£881,600; $1,423,772)
2.XI.98

This very rare design shows
12 flower sprigs, including
camellia, lotus and peony, on
the shoulders of the vase,
while the main body depicts
fruiting leafy branches,
including peach, grape and
lychee, above a narrow
classic scroll band above
the foot. The fruit sprays
and detailed borders are
finely painted, and have a
marked three-dimensional
quality. A similar example
can be seen in the Palace
Museum in Beijing.

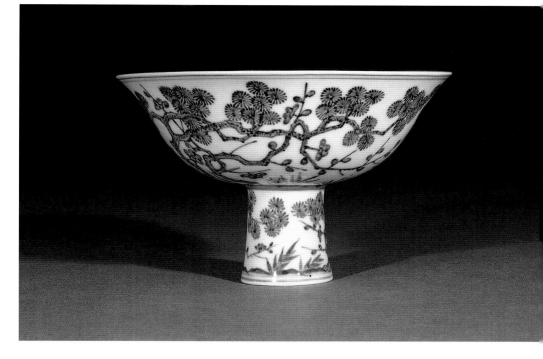

A Blue and White 'Three Friends' Stembowl

Four character mark and period of Xuande
Diameter 17.3 cm (6¼ in)
Hong Kong HK$7,500,000
(£581,395; $968,992) 2.XI.98

The 'Three Friends' featured in this design are blossoming prunus, a pine tree and clumps of bamboo. The design is a well-known subject of the Xuande period, but is rarely seen on stembowls. There are two known examples of stembowls featuring this design on the exterior, and one example of a bowl showing the unusual combination of *lingzhi* heads and bamboo encircling the 'Three Friends' on the interior, but the combination in this example appears to be unique. It is also rare to find the Xuande four-character mark inside the deep, hollow foot on the underside of the bowl.

A Blue and White 'Palace' Bowl

Ming Dynasty, six character mark and period of Chenghua
15.5 cm (6⅛ in)
Hong Kong HK$9,260,000
(£740,800; $1,196,382) 27.IV.99

This bowl is one of only ten recorded examples of its design. The design was developed during the Xuande period, but did not become popular until the reign of the Ming Emperor Chenghua (1465–87). It has Flowers of the Four Seasons on the inside around a sprig of chrysanthemum, with a gardenia scroll outside, and is perhaps the most varied and elaborate design known for palace bowls. This piece is known as the Sedgwick palace bowl, as it was in the collection of the great English collector Mrs Walter Sedgwick, and was sold through Sotheby's in 1968.

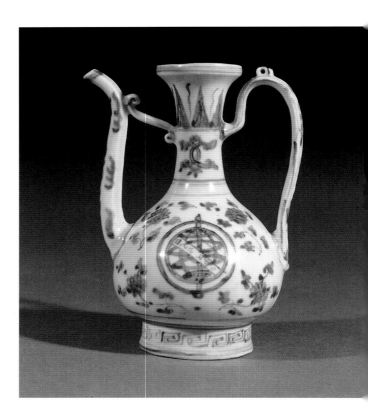

A Cloisonné Enamel Bombé Censer

Ming Dynasty, early 15th century
Height 20.2 cm (8 in)
London £320,500 ($516,005) 16.VI.99

A world record price for cloisonné enamels was established in 1999 by this rare piece from the McLaren Collection. One of the few important collections of Chinese cloisonné enamels in the West, it included fine pieces from most periods, particularly from the earliest beginnings in the Ming Dynasty (1368–1644), of which this is a notable example.

A Cizhou Sgraffiato
Meiping

Northern Song Dynasty, 960–1279
Height 30.5 cm (12 in), diameter 17.8 cm (7 in)
New York $530,500 (£318,300) 17.IX.98

This *meiping*, a type of vase with a very narrow neck originally designed to hold a branch of prunus, shows a design characteristic of Cizhou ware. This example is rare, belonging to a small group of Cizhou wares using two types of slip, usually decorated in bold designs in black on a white ground, often, as here, with large peony scrolls, which can be traced to the Guantai kilns in Ci County, Heibei Province.

A Blue and White 'Armillary Sphere' Ewer

Ming Dynasty, mark of Zhengde, c.1520–40
Height 18 cm (7⅛ in)
London £177,500 ($298,200) 18.XI.98

The armillary sphere was the personal device of King Emanuel I of Portugal (1469–1521) representing temporal power over his expanding empire. It has been suggested that most 'armillary sphere' pieces were produced during the Jiajing period at the behest of King Dom Joao III (1521–57). However, the ewer illustrated here is unique in reign mark and decoration and so becomes an important element in suggesting a Zhengde date for Sino-Portugese porcelain.

A 'Famille-rose' Vase (*Tianqiuping*)

Seal mark and period of Yongzheng
Height 51 cm (20⅛ in)
London £238,000 ($383,180)
16.VI.99

Dating from the Yongzheng period (1723–35), this vase is finely painted with luxurious herbaceous peonies in delicate shades of white, pink, iron-red and yellow. The pink and white enamels are drawn with such restraint as to reveal the bluish-white glaze underneath, giving the petals a gentle translucency.

A *Sancai*-glazed Pottery Camel and Foreign Rider

Tang Dynasty (AD 618–906)
84.5 by 67.3 cm (33¼ by 26½ in)
New York $261,000 (£159,210) 23.III.99

It is very rare to find such a large pottery camel and rider in this particularly attractive colour scheme. The powerfully modelled camel, which is arching its neck and appears to be braying, has a green, chestnut and straw blanket on its back. Seated between the humps is a foreign rider with a tall, peaked hat and exaggerated facial features, wearing a long chestnut jacket and trousers.

A *Huanghuali* Horseshoeback Armchair, *Quanyi*

16th/17th century
104.1 by 62.9 by 49.5 cm (41 by 24¾ by 19½ in)
New York $79,500 (£48,495) 23.III.99

This chair, which was purchased in Beijing before 1949, is part of a larger set of which several examples are known, including one in the Palace Museum, Beijing, and another in the collection of Robert H. Ellsworth. The chairs are distinguished by the boldly carved dragons on the splat, and also the dramatically curved crestrail and handgrips, features generally not found on horseshoeback chairs.

JAPANESE WORKS OF ART

Yokoyama Taikan

Pine Trees and Cranes
A pair of six-panel screens
(only one illustrated)
Ink, colours and gold leaf
on paper, 172.5 by 384 cm
(67 by 151⅛ in)
New York $442,500
(£261,075) 18.ⅠX.98

Yokoyama Taikan (1868–
1958) is perhaps one of
the most recognized
20th-century Japanese artists
associated with *Nihonga*
(Japanese-style painting).
Born at the close of the Edo
period and the beginning of
the Meiji period, Taikan's
career mirrors the great
transitions of his time.
Japan began to cast aside
its traditions in favour of all

things Western and the
artistic community looked
West for inspiration. The
merging of new influences
with traditional Japanese art
produced the new genre,
Nihonga. The subject here, of
cranes and pine trees, is a
classic Japanese allusion to
longevity and is presented
using elements from various
schools of Japanese painting.

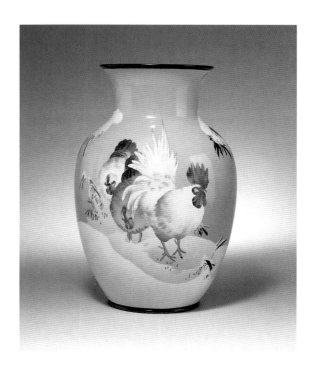

Cloisonné Enamel Vase by Namikawa Sosuke

Late Meiji period
(1868–1912)
Height 42 cm (16½ in)
New York $51,750 (£31,568)
24.ⅠⅠⅠ.99

Throughout his career
Namikawa Sosuke
(1847–1910) developed his
enamelling technique to
emulate the works of
painters and book
illustrators. This vase is an
exceptional example of his

work; the subject of a
cockerel, while not unusual
among the patterns for
Sosuke's cloisonné enamel
trays, is not typical. In
addition, a vase of this size is
rare for this artist.

Kitagawa Utamaro
The Awabi Fishers
Signed *Utamaro hitsu*
Triptych: right hand sheet
36.5 by 24.7 cm (14⅜ by
9¾ in); centre 36.5 by
24.2 cm (14⅜ by 9½ in);
left 36.9 by 24.3 cm
(14½ by 9½ in)
London £172,000 ($273,480)
17.VI.99

In the right hand sheet of this
triptych a young woman has
come to buy *awabi*, a type of
marine snail, just retrieved
by the girl in the traditional
red skirt worn by these fisher
women. She grips between
her teeth a *tegane* (crow-bar)
with which she has prised the
seafood from the rocks. The
image of the basket is

repeated in the centre panel,
where a young woman
suckles a boy as she combs
her hair. The final sheet of the
triptych shows two girls on a
rock. This is one of the most
widely known and admired of
all Japanese figure prints and
examples in the same
condition as the one
illustrated here are very few.

PRE-COLUMBIAN ART

A Mayan dignitary
Jaina, Late Classic
c. AD 550–950
Height 26.7 cm (10½ in)
New York $200,500
(£124,310) 2.VI.99

The Pre-Columbian tradition
of ceramic figurines reached
an especially high level of
sophistication with the
Mayan hand-modelled and
mould-made figures from
Jaina Island and the coastal
region of Campeche. These
sculptures, which give details
of the daily life and rituals of
the Maya people, represent
deities, men, women and
animals. Details of clothing
and physical features are
carefully portrayed,
bestowing the figures with
stature and presence. The
example illustrated is one of
the most expressive known
to exist. As a portrait of a
mature court ruler, he is
depicted in a commanding
posture and is embellished
with the attributes of
distinguished rank.

AMERICAN INDIAN ART

A Kwakiutl Wood Shaman figure
Height 141 cm (55½ in)
New York $145,500
(£90,210) 26.v.99

The shaman or medicine man was a powerful and important figure amongst the Native American tribes of the northwest coast. Often the most revered person in the community, the shaman used his power to cure sickness and, on occasion, to cause it. He entertained and frightened people with magic, possibly in competition with other medicine men. This carving, with its curiously exaggerated crown of bear claws and imposing grimace, was probably used as a marker at the front of a house or ceremonial lodge, to convey the strength and mystical force of its owner.

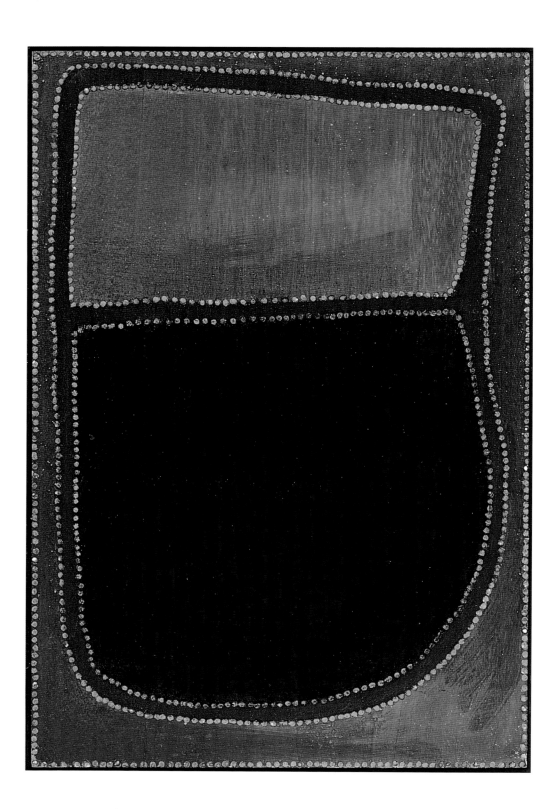

Rover Thomas (Joolama)
Wolf Creek Crater 1986
Natural earth pigments and
natural binder (bush gum)
on plywood, 90 by 60 cm
(35½ by 23⅝ in)
Melbourne A$107,000
(£43,870; $70,620) 28.VI.99
Property from the Holmes à
Court Collection, Heytesbury

Rover Thomas's work
transformed the indigenous
art produced in the East
Kimberley region of Western
Australia. Traditionally,
images were painted on
boards or took sculptural
forms and two or three of
these would be used to
accompany ceremonial
performances, or palga. In
contrast, Thomas's palga
was saturated with paintings
which spanned a huge range
of subject matter. As Kim
Akerman has noted, Thomas
(c. 1926–98) also 'introduced
significant changes to their
content, dispensing with the
thread-cross work that
adorned many Kimberley
dancing boards and
representing images instead
in map or aerial form'. This
painting depicts the sacred
site *Kandimalal* (Wolf Creek
Meteor Crater), which was
created by a mythological
Rainbow Serpent.

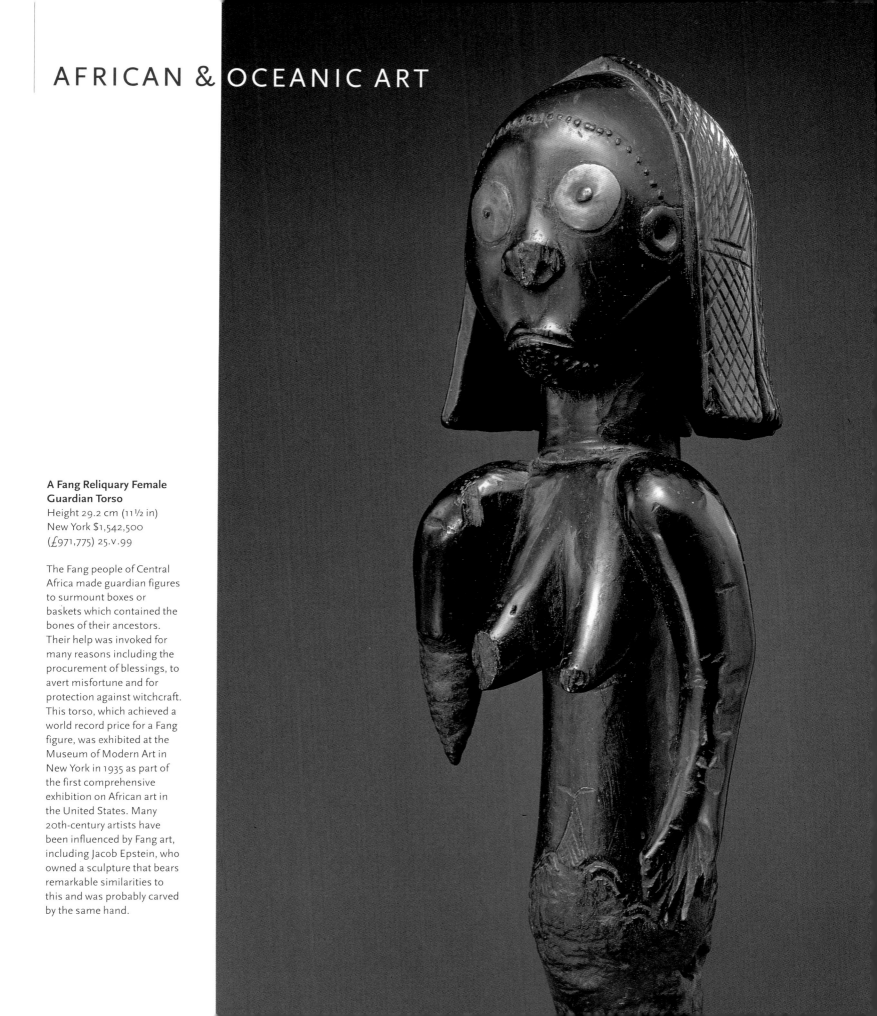

AFRICAN & OCEANIC ART

A Fang Reliquary Female Guardian Torso
Height 29.2 cm (11½ in)
New York $1,542,500
(£971,775) 25.V.99

The Fang people of Central Africa made guardian figures to surmount boxes or baskets which contained the bones of their ancestors. Their help was invoked for many reasons including the procurement of blessings, to avert misfortune and for protection against witchcraft. This torso, which achieved a world record price for a Fang figure, was exhibited at the Museum of Modern Art in New York in 1935 as part of the first comprehensive exhibition on African art in the United States. Many 20th-century artists have been influenced by Fang art, including Jacob Epstein, who owned a sculpture that bears remarkable similarities to this and was probably carved by the same hand.

ANTIQUITIES

**A Black Chlorite Figure of
a Mythological Hero**
Bactria or Eastern Persia
c. 2,200–2,000 BC
Height 11.4 cm (4½ in)
New York $800,000
(£496,000) 5.VI.99

This stocky and muscular
figure carries an offering
container under his right arm
and wears a skirt which has
drilled circular pendants that
were at one time inlaid. The
strings connecting these
pendants to the belt are
inlaid with gold foil and it is
possible that the pendants
were in fact seals that
represented membership of
a particular clan or tribe. The
scaly body, perhaps
representing hair, and the
beast-like expression suggest
possible links with the
mythical giant Humbaba,
who was defeated by the hero
Gilgamesh. A figure with
similar features is in the
collections of the Louvre.

A Late Gothic Gilt and Painted Lindenwood 'Heilige Sippe' (Holy Kinship) altar
c. 1500
Central panel 163.8 by 123.8 cm (64½ by 48¾ in); wings 163.8 by 62.2 cm (64½ by 24½ in)
New York $200,500 (£118,295) 23.1x.98

The central panel of this altar depicts Mary crowned and holding the Christ Child, who is handing an orb to St Anne. On the wall above are the three legendary husbands of St Anne including Joachim, the father of the Virgin Mary; John the Baptist stands on their left. The full-length figures flanking this scene are the Sts Margaret of Antioch and Catherine of Alexandria. The side panels show other scenes from the life of Christ. The drapery and faces, in conjunction with the carved gable, are close in style to that of an altar in the Isabella Stewart Gardner Museum.

An Ivory Group of the Madonna and Child
Mosan, second quarter 13th century
31.4 by 10.5 by 10.2 cm (12⅜ by 4⅛ by 4 in)
New York $662,500 (£404,125) 29.1.99

The dating of this group has been aided by several unusual features, in particular the bare lower leg of the Child. This links the group to works assigned to the Meuse valley in the 13th century. The origin of the bare-legged Child has been traced to Byzantium, and is said to draw attention to Christ's physical presence, and earthly sacrifice. Other features are Byzantine, while the design on the Virgin's clothes is characteristic of 13th-century France.

A Group of Three Oak Figures

English, mid 15th century, mounted on later oak board
Height 109 cm (43 in)
London £111,500 ($176,170)
7.VII.99

This group shows a knight in armour on the left, with a knife on a belt round his waist, and a page on the right. The central figure is possibly a nobleman, and both he and the page wear short-waisted tunics with prominent codpieces. The figures may have been supporters for a tomb or figures in a secular setting as they are carved in the round and therefore meant to be viewed from all sides. Medieval sculpture has survived very rarely in England due to the violent religious and political upheavals of the 16th and 17th centuries.

A French White Marble Group of Saturn Devouring One of His Children

Before 1699, by Simon Hurtrelle
64 by 22 by 24 cm
(25 by 8½ by 9½ in)
London £62,000 ($99,200)
8.VI.99

Simon Hurtrelle (1648–1724) studied at the Academy of Saint Luc in Rome and returned to France around 1682 to work for Louis XIV at Versailles. He became a member of the Académie Royale in 1687 and an assistant professor in 1706. It has recently come to light that this group was exhibited at the 1699 Salon. Saturn was the Roman god of agriculture and can be identified with the Greek God Cronus. Gaea (Mother Earth) had prophesied that Cronus would be usurped by one of his children, so he ate them to prevent this. The prophecy finally came true: when Zeus was born Cronus was tricked by being given a stone wrapped in swaddling clothes, while Zeus was saved and later overthrew his father.

NINETEENTH-CENTURY SCULPTURE

Charles-Henri-Joseph Cordier
A pair of porte-torchères of La femme Fellah and La femme Abyssinienne, c. 1869, both signed *C. Cordier*
Onyx, marble, bronze, silvered and gilt-bronze and enamel, each 175 cm (69 in)
London £573,500 ($952,010)
26.XI.98

These two figures, which achieved a world record price for a single lot of 19th-century sculpture, show both Cordier's interest in anthropology and his innovative use of materials. Cordier made his final major foreign expedition – to Egypt – in 1865, and subsequently concentrated on larger and more ambitious projects. In these two figures he makes characteristically striking use of highly polished onyx, gilding and silvering, with touches of enamel. It is thought that the figures are related to a *Fontaine Egyptienne* shown at the 1869 Salon, but known only from photographs.

Sir George James Frampton, RA
Peter Pan
Inscribed *GF* and *PP* within a circle, dated 1913
Bronze, height overall 60.4 cm (23¼ in)
New York $60,250 (£37,355)
5.V.99

This piece is a smaller version of the statue that stands in Kensington Gardens, London, which was given to the public by an anonymous donor in 1911. The statue stands on the spot where, in J. M. Barrie's book of the same name, Peter Pan landed for his nightly visits and where he plays his pipe to the spirits of the children who have played there.

ENGLISH FURNITURE

A Pair of George II Mahogany Arm Chairs from Newhailes House, Scotland
With the original Royal Aubusson tapestry covers by Pierre Mage
c. 1750
New York $233,500
(£137,765) 24.x.98

Although the maker of these chairs is not known, they are stylistically related to a large suite of furniture made for the 4th Earl of Shaftsbury for St Giles's House, Dorset. Pierre Mage, born into a family of tapestry weavers, worked for the Aubusson factory between 1697 and 1747. The Aubusson tapestry created for these arm chairs boasts strapwork cartouches interwoven with scrolling leaves and brightly coloured summer flowers on a claret background. The cartouches on the backs have a displayed peacock or an exotic crane and the seats are decorated with a deer or fox.

A Large Pair of Chinese Mirror Paintings
Second half 18th century, 179 by 114 cm (5 ft 10½ in by 3 ft 5 in)
London £287,500 ($448,500) 9.VII.99

The majority of Chinese mirror paintings of this date depict the landscape in summer season, as is the case with one of this pair; but it is rare to find an autumn scene as represented by the other example. The large size and thickness of the glass would indicate glass of French manufacture, and it is possible the mirrors were supplied through the agency of the Compagnie des Indes, which, in common with other European trading companies, maintained an important presence at the port of Canton.

**A Set of Four George II
Fruitwood and Needlework
Covered Side Chairs**

c. 1735
London £56,500 ($88,140)
9.VII.99

The present set of four side
chairs, with their remarkable
floral needlework covers,
originally formed part of a
larger suite of seat furniture
including four further side
chairs and a matching settee.
The needlework covers were
made during the 1730s by
Penelope Hyde of Hyde Hall,

Cheshire, an example of
which is in the Metropolitan
Museum in New York.

A George III Gilt-metal-mounted Satinwood, Tulipwood and Rosewood Dressing Commode
Attributed to Henry Hill of Marlborough, *c.* 1775, 87 by 125.1 by 64.8 cm (34¼ in by 4 ft 1¼ in by 25½ in)
New York $90,500 (£53,395)
23.x.98

This elaborately decorated dressing commode is one of a small group of similarly ornamented commodes and pembroke tables which are attributed to the cabinet-maker Henry Hill and date from 1741 to his death in 1778. Most of his known clients appear to have resided near Marlborough in Wiltshire, and included the 9th Duke of Somerset, Arabella Calley and Lord Delaval. The present commode is identical in form to three other recorded examples, two of these being slightly smaller and all sharing the same gilt mounts and lustrous satinwood veneer.

CONTINENTAL FURNITURE

A Louis XV Chinoserie Clock
Signed *JULIEN LE ROY DE LA SOCIETE DES ARTS A PARIS*
30 by 36 cm (11¾ by 14⅛ in)
Monaco FF1,222,500
(£120,681; $192,216)
18.VI.99

Julian II Le Roy (1686–1759) was received as a master in Paris in 1713 and is one of the most celebrated clockmakers of 18th-century France. He brought precise methods to Parisian watchmaking, similar to those of his English contemporaries. Le Roy was president of the Society of Arts and was awarded lodgement in the Louvre Palace from 1739, with the title 'Horloger Ordinaire du Roi'. The type of lacquer on this clock, which was fashionable in the late 1730s, is truly an enamel and imitates Chinese and Japanese lacquer work. It was perfected by the Martin family who for two generations held a virtual monopoly over the technique.

A Pair of Italian White Marble and Polychrome Marble Inlaid Console Tables
Neapolitan, second or third quarter 18th century
125 by 81 by 48 cm (4 ft 9½ in by 2 ft 8 in by 1 ft 7 in)
London £243,500 ($409,080)
16.XII.98

Although these putti, in the form of sea creatures with entwined tails, may recall earlier Baroque ideas such as those practised by Bernini in Rome and Parodi in Genoa, the origin of the present console tables should be found in Naples in the 18th century, where several sculptors used polychrome marbles in their work. Here the putti support a marble top, their arms draped with berried laurel leaf swags and decorated with embossed *giallo antico* bracelets of polychrome marbles.

**The Palazzo Carrega
Cataldi Sofas**
Two pairs of Italian carved
giltwood sofas, Genoese,
c. 1740–44
Width 284 cm (9 ft 3¾ in)
London £195,500 ($328,440)
16.XII.98
From the Collection of Count
Volpi di Misurata

The Palazzo Carrega Cataldi
has a distinguished history
and originally belonged to
one of the wealthiest
Genoese Renaissance
families, the Pallavicinos. It
was purchased in 1704 by
Filippo Carrega who, with his
son, undertook considerable
renovations to the palace,
including the construction
and decoration of the
famous Gilded Gallery, which
is still in existence. This awe-
inspiring room, with its
exuberant gilded stuccoes
typifying the froth and excess
of the luxuriant rococo style,
was conceived, possibly
together with the rest of the
panelling and furniture, by
Lorenzo De Ferrari between
1743 and 1744. The present
sofas originally stood below
four large mirrors on the two
long walls.

A Louis XVI Ormolu and Sèvres Porcelain-mounted Table

c. 1778, Martin Carlin
71.8 by 64.1 by 36.2 cm
(28¼ by 25¼ by 14¼ in)
New York $2,972,500
(£1,783,500) 5.xi.98

Flower-painted porcelain was extremely popular in the late 18th century, but this type of furniture with elaborate ormulu mounts was difficult to make, and required detailed, lengthy planning. Indeed, the making of large plaques like the one at the table's centre was expensive and skilled work, as many of them were damaged during the firing process. Although this table has no signature to show the maker, a little of the wood on the underside has been gouged out deliberately, probably by the dealer to conceal the identity of the maker. However, the table's similarity to another in the Gulbenkian Museum in Lisbon, and a drawing in the Metropolitan Museum in New York, prove the maker's identity without doubt.

A Louis XVI Ebony Bureau Plat by Philippe-Claude Montigny

Stamped *Montigny*
74 by 145.5 by 72.5 cm
(29⅛ by 57¼ by 28½ in)
Monaco FF3,532,500
(£348,716; $555,424)
18.VI.99
Formerly in the Collection of the Duchess of Mouchy

Philippe-Claude Montigny (1734–1800) was the son of a furniture maker who lived in the Faubourg Saint-Antoine. His father's shop, where he was apprenticed, was within walking distance of the Bastille. Montigny also collaborated with his cousin René Dubois, whose prosperous business was instrumental in the birth of neo-classicism. Montigny specialized in the restoration and resale of Boulle furniture of earlier date, almost certainly working in that capacity for the dealer Julliot. Not only did he restore Boulle furniture but he also copied it and sometimes realized pastiches, using Boulle panels set in the neo-classical ebony structure.

An Italian Baroque Inlaid Marble Table Top

Early 17th century
Length 2.84 m (9 ft 4 in),
width 1.37 m (4 ft 6 in)
New York $2,752,500
(£1,651,500) 5.xi.98

This massive table top is composed of lapis lazuli, various marbles and other hard stones and is decorated with military emblems. The central oval is of *breccia Quintilina*, and the table's decorations are mainly composed of militaria, including flags, lances, shields, axes, quivers with arrows, and cuirasses. Research by Alvar González-Palacios has demonstrated that the table top is the pendant to a similar example once owned by Don Rodrigo Calderón (1576–1621), an important figure in the court of King Philip III of Spain, now in the Museo del Prado in Madrid. Consequently, this table top can be dated to early 17th-century Rome, a city that is the source of a vast array of marbles and coloured stones, where the art of inlaid decoration in these media originated.

NINETEENTH-CENTURY FURNITURE

Four American Aesthetic Movement Brass-mounted Oak Side Chairs
Herter Brothers, New York, c. 1880
New York $101,500 (£63,945)
24.VI.99
The Collection of William H. Vanderbilt, New York, New York

Gustave Herter was a German cabinetmaker who arrived in New York in 1848. He formed a partnership with his brother Christian in 1864, and the brothers went on to design entire interiors as well as single commissions for grand houses. These four chairs are part of a set of 18, of which only six are known to survive. They were carved in oak to complement the Renaissance-style oak panelling of the dining room of 640 Fifth Avenue, New York, owned by William H. Vanderbilt, and were originally upholstered in embossed leather. Vanderbilt (1821–85) was a financier widely considered to be the wealthiest man of his day.

A Red Japanned Day Bed
Gabriel Viardot, Paris, dated *1887*, signed *G. Viardot, Paris 1887*
180 by 83 cm (67 by 31 in)
London £34,500 ($58,995)
2.X.98

Gabriel Viardot specialized in exotic furniture and advertised as a *createur des meubles dans le genre chinois*

et japonais (a creator of furniture in the Chinese and Japanese style). Chinese and Vietnamese styles strongly influenced Viardot; Vietnam was one of France's principal colonies and considerable quantities of furniture were imported into France from the Far East, in particular from Canton and Hanoi.

C.C. Hofmann

The Berks County Almshouse, Hospital and Lunatic Asylum
Signed and inscribed
C. Hofmann, dated *1865*
Ink and watercolour on
paper, 60 by 103.2 cm
(23⅝ by 40⅝ in)
New York $112,500 (£67,500)
17.1.99

Few facts are known about Charles Hofmann, a remarkable 19th-century itinerant painter, who came to the United States in 1860 when he was 39 years old. Hofmann was known to have sought refuge in three almshouses along Pennsylvania's Schuylkill River. This rare watercolour, one of two of this particular subject known to have been painted by Hofmann, documents the Berks County Almshouse, Hospital and Lunatic Asylum. While staying at the almshouses, Hofmann painted views of the institutions for members of the administrative staffs, the politically appointed county board of directors and local tradesmen. In this work, the expansive bird's-eye view documents the complex from the front and includes the surrounding buildings that supported the poor people of the county. Today, the work remains as a classic example of the naïve style of 19th-century American folk paintings.

Bill Traylor

Bird and Man
1939–42
Pencil and tempera on cardboard, 43.8 by 27.9 cm (17¼ by 11 in)
New York $46,000 (£27,600) 17.1.99

Bill Traylor, a self-taught African-American artist from Benton, Alabama, began drawing at the advanced age of 85. Born into slavery in 1854, Traylor's experiences included his work as a plantation labourer, a blacksmith, a basket maker, a poleman for a surveying crew and a shoe factory worker. Late in his life, he moved to Montgomery, where he could be seen daily sitting in front of the local pool hall drawing and painting on bits of scrap paper and cardboard. As a keen observer of the world, he produced a remarkable number of whimsical works that captured the essence of his memories in a universal and timeless manner. This work, bordering on the abstract, is a brilliant example of Traylor's unique visual expression.

A Moulded Copper and Zinc Greyhound Weathervane by J. Howard and Company

West Bridgewater, Massachusetts, mid-19th century
54.6 by 83.8 cm (21½ by 33 in)
New York $101,500 (£60,900) 17.1.99

A need to predict the weather has long interested man. One of the first meteorological instruments, devised for the purpose of determining the direction of the wind, was the weathervane. American weathervanes, initially derived from European examples, were the first significant form of American vernacular sculpture, and many of their makers became famous in their own time. Mounted atop a cupola or roof, weathervanes in such popular forms as roosters, horses, mermaids or Indians were a handsome and useful addition to American houses and barns. This swell-bodied figure of a standing greyhound is the only known weathervane of its kind to have come on to the market. Although the maker is unknown, its rare form alone was enough to inspire fierce competition among Americana collectors.

A Chippendale Figured Mahogany Serpentine-front Marble-top Pier Table
Boston, Massachusetts,
1755–75
74.9 by 139.7 by 66 cm
(29½ in by 4 ft 7 in by 26 in)
New York $882,500
(£529,500) 17.1.99

According to books detailing the furniture used in the United States during the second half of the 18th century, this table with its grey-veined marble top is of a popular type. Fashionable Colonial houses usually owned a pair of such tables, which were covered with damask cloths and used primarily for placing food on. J.C. Loudon dictates in his *Encyclopaedia* that the tables should be arranged on each side of the room, hot foods being placed on one and cold on the other. Stylistically, the table shows its English Georgian antecedents, as well as contemporary Eastern Massachusetts features. The table was recently rediscovered in a consignment shop in the greater San Francisco area.

A Federal Satinwood- and ivory-inlaid Figured Mahogany Tambour Secretary

Attributed to John and Thomas Seymour, Boston, Massachusetts, c. 1800
120.7 by 95.3 by 49.5 cm (47½ by 37½ by 19½ in)
New York $299,500 (£179,700) 17.1.99

John Seymour was an English cabinetmaker who moved to the United States in 1784. Initially he had difficulty in competing with the flourishing native craftsmen, so to distinguish his furniture from theirs, he introduced the George III style to the country, now known as 'Federal' style. He also concentrated on the type of furniture that would appeal to women, who, with increased wealth and literacy, were consequently more occupied with reading and letter writing. This secretary, with its fashionably coloured 'sky blew' pigeonholes, was evidently for this market, and was made in partnership with Seymour's son Thomas.

A Queen Anne Carved and Figured Parcel-gilt Mahogany Bonnet-top Secretary Bookcase

Wethersfield, Connecticut, 1740–60
243.3 by 90.2 by 55.9 cm (8 ft by 35½ in by 22 in)
New York $497,500 (£298,500) 17.1.99

This secretary bookcase has unusual vertical proportions. The top has three gilded flame finials and a swan's-neck pediment above arched panelled doors, which open to reveal four tiers of pigeonholes, five short drawers and candleslides. The beautifully carved fans on the upper middle and lower sections help unify the overall design. While most furniture made in Connecticut during this period is of cherrywood, the cabinetmaker chose a more expensive imported mahogany for this piece. The bookcase appears to retain its original finish, finials and cast-brass hardware.

OPPOSITE

One of a Pair of Gilt-metal-mounted Böttger Porcelain Vases and Covers
c.1715, modelled by Johann Jakob Irminger
Heights 51.5 cm (20¼ in) and 51 cm (20 in)
London £133,500 ($221,610)
24.XI.98

Listed in the 1710 personnel lists of the Meissen factory as 'responsible for inventions and new designs', Johann Jakob Irminger was closely involved with the manufactory in the first decade of its existence. These particular vases, designed by Irminger, were presented by Augustus the Strong, Elector of Hanover and King of Poland, to Vittorio Amadeo II of Sardinia. The two men became firm friends in 1688 when Vittorio Amadeo, then Duke of Savoy, had sheltered the young Friedrich August when the outbreak of war disrupted his tour of Italy. In return for these vases Vittorio Amadeo sent Sardinian tapestries.

***E finita la musica*: A Mintons *Pâte-sur-pâte* Vase**
c. 1900
Height 64.8 cm (25½ in)
New York $54,625 (£34,414)
24.VI.99

Pâte-sur-pâte is a technique of surface decoration where the design is created from multiple layers of thinly applied white or coloured clay slip. This unusually large vase was decorated by Louis Marc Emmanuel Solon, one of the greatest exponents of the technique, who worked at the Mintons factory in Stoke-on-Trent, England between 1870 and 1904. It is one of six known vases of this form decorated by Solon, the most widely published being the pair known as *Vintage* and *La pêche* which were exhibited at the Paris Universal Exhibition of 1889.

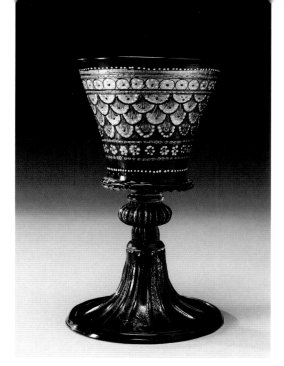

A Venetian Enamelled and Gilt Blue-tinted Goblet
*c.*1475–1500
Height 20.7 cm (8⅛ in)
London £144,500 ($244,205)
15.XII.98

This glass, and one other, formed part of the contents of Derwydd Mansion in West Wales which were sold by Sotheby's in 1998 (page 186). The house dates back to the 16th century and has passed through the female line and therefore the hands of many families. The history of the mansion has been as changeable as its ownership; in 1670 it was one of the largest seats in the area but, as often happens when heiresses attract richer husbands, the house became tenanted, a secondary house to a new seat built ten miles away. The house would have fallen into disrepair had it not been rescued in the 1880s, after which much was added to its contents. Although these goblets may have passed through the same history as the house it is far more likely that they were acquired at this time.

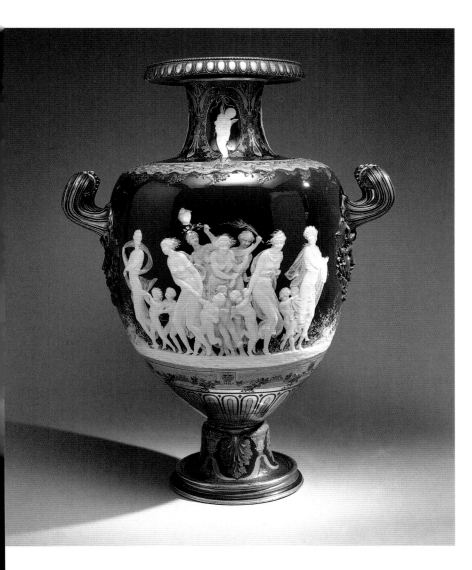

A Clichy Concentric Millefiori Moss Ground Weight
19th century
Diameter 7.4 cm (2⅞ in)
New York $96,000 (£59,520)
16.VI.99

Scattered millefiori canes are a typical feature of these much sought-after moss ground weights. The concentric arrangement of canes displayed in this particular piece is, however, unusual. It is one of over 100 paperweights comprising the renowned collection of F. Regnault and Frances C.D. Fairchild. Ren and Frances purchased their first weights in 1950 at an auction in Philadelphia and continued to search for some of the finest examples from the US and abroad to build their much treasured collection.

A Tiffany Poppy Filigree Floor Lamp

1899–1928, shade impressed
TIFFANY STUDIOS/NEW YORK,
base impressed *TIFFANY
STUDIOS/NEW YORK/3136*
Favrile glass and bronze
Height 201 cm (6 ft 7 in),
diameter 61 cm (24 in)
New York $607,500
(£364,500) 5.x11.98

This lamp is a variation of an
existing Tiffany Studios
design, made to a client's
special order. The design
combines the characteristics
of both the standard poppy
filigree lamp and lamps with
irregular lower borders. The
domed shade shows poppy
blossoms in various states of
development, with some
blossom centres overlaid on
the exterior of the shade with
pierced bronze filigree. The
lower border is composed of
furling poppy leaves, again
overlaid with pierced bronze
filigree. The mottled
green-brown lamp base
shows radiating leaves and is
raised on four petal-form
feet. No other examples of
this lamp are known to exist.

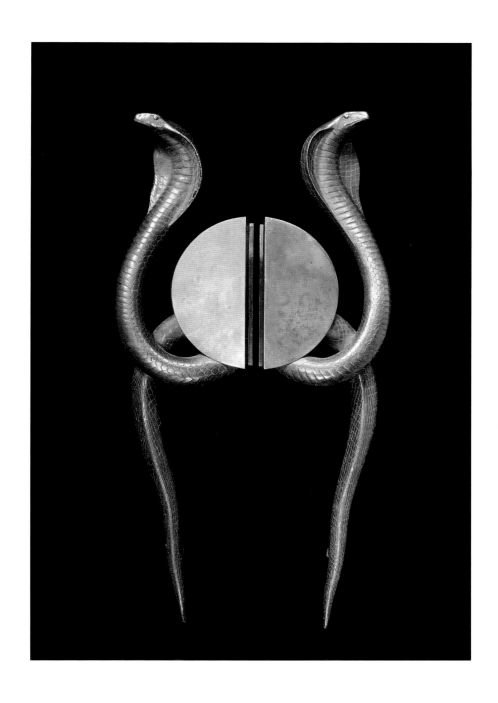

A Pair of Serpent Door Handles by Edgar Brandt
c. 1925, each stamped
E. Brandt
Brown patinated bronze
Height 92 cm (36¼ in)
London £80,700 ($129,927)
1.IV.99

Edgar Brandt (1880–1960) was born in France and set up his studio in 1919. He had his own section at the 1925 Exposition and was recognized as a master craftsman in wrought iron, making doors, gates, furniture, screens and grilles.

These bronze door handles feature serpents' bodies decorated with a pattern of scales and twisted into a loop. The semi-circular holders on to which they are mounted are faintly marked 'Pull' on either side.

CARPETS AND RUGS

A Safavid Voided Silk Velvet, Metal Thread Strip and Bouclé Figural Velvet Panel
North Persia, possibly Qazvin, last third 16th century
156 by 137 cm (5 ft 2 in by 4 ft 6 in)
London £793,500 ($1,356,885) 14.x.98

Many elements of this highly important panel's decoration mirror developments in the art of Persian book illustration. This is particularly apparent in the depiction of the human figures; prior to *c*.1550 Persian painting referred to specific incidents in literature accompanied by appropriate portions of text, calligraphy thus being an integral part of the whole. Between *c*.1550 and *c*.1600 the images took on a more generic meaning, for example 'Lovers in a Landscape' or 'The Pastoral Idyll', making a pictorial language in which text was unnecessary. With the divorcing of images from a specific incident the use of figures in repetitive patterns became acceptable. This velvet panel, which achieved the highest ever auction price for an oriental textile or carpet, exemplifies this tendency, showing an exchange in a stylized landscape, but without narrative context.

A Tabriz Carpet
Northwest Persia, *c.* 1900
696 by 452 cm (22 ft 10 in by
14 ft 10 in)
New York $206,000
(£129,780) 7.IV.99

Tabriz in Northern Iran has a
long and varied history; its
origins are believed to be at
some point between
AD 224 and AD 651. During
the 12th and 13th centuries it
was ruled by the Moguls and
with the waning of their
influence the town was
sacked by Tamberlane. In
the 15th century the town
declined after the Safavid
dynasty moved the capital
of the region to a more
defensible site, and it was
not until the second half of
the 19th century that the
region returned to prosperity
as a trading post on the route
from the Iranian interior to
the West. Definite
information about the carpet
production of the area prior
to the 16th century is limited,
but it is possible that Tabriz
carpets were in Europe in the
15th century. During the 16th
century the region flourished
under the Safavids and the
area is still a major carpet
producer. This fine example
from *c.* 1900 illustrates the
proficiency of the weavers
of Tabriz.

EUROPEAN TAPESTRIES

A Bruges Gamepark Tapestry
Late 16th century
178 by 460 cm (5 ft 10 in by 15 ft 1 in)
New York $134,500 (£82,012) 29.1.99
Property from the Estate of Mr and Mrs William H. Crocker, San Francisco, California, 1937

At the centre of this tapestry is a palace of Italian design, surrounded by an ornamental garden and cut hedge. On the lake surrounding it swim swans and other wildfowl, while the foreground features a verdant landscape. On foot and horseback hunters pursue their game and a fisherman makes a successful catch. A richly decorated border surrounds the scene, with cartouches, strapwork, flowers and fruit.

The Story of Artemisia
A set of eight metalthread tapestries from a set woven for Henri IV, Paris, Faubourg Saint-Marcel, pre 1610, after Henri Lerambert and Laurent Guyot, the borders with royal arms, emblems and monograms, all with royal fleur-de-lys and Paris factory mark and weaver's mark *FM*
London £93,900 ($148,362) 7.VII.99

These tapestries appear in an inventory compiled upon the death of the 4th Earl of Carlisle, Castle Howard, Yorkshire, in 1759, but it is not known how or when the Earl acquired them. They were subsequently sent to Naworth Castle. The series was based on an epic poem written by Nicolas Houel in 1562 entitled *Histoire de la Royne Arthemise*. In turn, this was based on the story of Artemisia, queen of Caria, who was left to educate her young son Lygdamis after the death of his father Mausolus. The story served as a parallel for the duties of Catherine de Medici, widow of Henri II, who served as regent to Charles IX, and, after her, Marie de Medici, widow of Henri IV, as regent to Louis XIII.

JEWELLERY

A Diamond Ring
Harry Winston
Geneva SF3,083,500
(£1,268,930; $2,042,052)
19.V.99

Claw-set with a marquise-shaped diamond mounted in platinum, this ring is signed *Winston*. The diamond, weighing 49.62 carats, is of the finest 'D' colour; it is flanked by tapered baguette diamonds.

A Diamond Necklace
Cartier, London, *c.* 1950
Geneva SF4,293,500
(£1,766,872; $2,843,377)
19.V.99

The five largest stones in this necklace weigh 63.04 carats making up just part of the total of 23 claw-set brilliant cut diamonds. They are alternated with collet-set marquise-shaped stones and the clasp is accented with baquette diamonds. All stones are mounted in platinum and the necklace is signed *Cartier, London*.

A Fancy Coloured Diamond Ring

Geneva SF4,850,500
(£2,099,783; $3,540,510)
19.XI.98

The three coloured diamonds in this setting were each sold individually, the figure above being their combined total. The pear-shaped Fancy Intense orange-yellow, weighing 7.11 carats, the pear-shaped stone of Fancy Intense blue colour and the final stone of Fancy Intense purple-pink, cut with a modified step-cut, are mounted in a simple platinum band.

A Pair of Diamond Earclips

New York $1,487,500
(£922,250) 13.IV.99

The two round diamonds weigh 12.64 and 12.13 carats respectively, and are mounted in platinum. Each of the stones possesses the most sought-after qualities in the 'Four Cs' of diamond assessment. The Cs stand for cut, colour, clarity and carat weight, and these diamonds are colourless and flawless, and of an unusually large size. The Gemological Institute of America has deemed the symmetry and polish of the stones 'excellent'. Usually rough diamonds are cut with an eye to economy, so that each rough yields the greatest possible number of diamonds, but here the cutter has sacrificed a large amount of rough – which might have been used to create diamonds of lesser quality – to achieve perfection in two large, round brilliants.

A Fancy Dark Grey-blue Diamond and Diamond Ring

Hong Kong HK$2,000,000
(£160,000; $258,397)
28.IV.99

Ten pear-shaped diamonds surround this 4.32-carat Fancy dark grey-blue diamond, the whole mounted in platinum. Blue diamonds were first heard of in 1669, when Jean Baptiste Tavernier sold a 112-carat blue diamond to Louis XIV. Blue diamonds owe their colour to the trace element boron, the amount present determining the depth of blue in the diamond.

A Diamond Necklace

Signed *Van Cleef & Arpels*, numbered *NY 9843*
New York, *c.* 1950
Length approximately 38 cm (15 in)
New York $387,500
(£240,250) 13.IV.99

The centre supports nine flexible fringes of baguette diamonds, each anchored by a briolette diamond drop, suspended from a loop attached to single rows of baguette diamonds. The whole set, with 309 baguette diamonds weighing 28.46 carats and nine briolette diamonds weighing 35.86 carats, is mounted in platinum.

An Emerald and Diamond Aigrette

Early 19th century
New York $200,500
(£118,295) 20.X.98

The emeralds and diamonds making up this feather-shaped aigrette are set in silver and gold. Aigrettes are typically hat or hair ornaments made to support a feather or designed in the form of a jewelled feather, as here. They were first seen in the 17th century, and came into vogue again in the 19th and early 20th centuries. This example was, in this century, given by the Portuguese Count of Anadìa to his wife on the occasion of their wedding and remained in the family until its sale.

OPPOSITE

A Diamond Necklace

Signed *Petochi*, *c.* 1900
Length 53.3 cm (21 in)
New York $442,500
(£261,075) 20.X.98
Property of a Member of a European Royal Family

This rivière is composed of 43 collet-set old European-cut diamonds graduating in size, completed by a rosette clasp of seven diamonds, altogether weighing approximately 93.00 carats, mounted in platinum and accented with 44 small old European-cut diamonds set in between the larger stones. The diamonds come from the collection of Queen Margherita and were remounted by Petochi in the 1930s for the then Crown Princess Marie Josée of Italy. Petochi, which still makes jewellery in Rome, had recently been appointed supplier to the Royal family.

An Emerald and Diamond Corsage Ornament/Tiara

Mid 19th century
London £62,000 ($103,540)
3.XII.98

This tiara was part of the collection of jewels belonging to Duke G. de Leuchtenburg who was the great-grandson of Napoleon's wife, the Empress Joséphine. Designed as a spray of flowers set throughout with rose and cushion-shaped diamonds and decorated with variously cut emeralds, this important piece is housed in a case stamped with the crown of the Imperial House of Bonaparte.

A Jadeite Bead Necklace, with Art Deco Clasps
(detail), *c.* 1925
Overall length approximately
78 cm (29¼ in)
Hong Kong HK$6,620,000
(£529,600; $855,297)
28.IV.99

Together with the extra dash of colour from the Art Deco clasps, this necklace is a striking combination of the most traditional form of Chinese jewellery and the most exciting style of the orientalist Art Deco period. Its beads are *mei hua lu* (plum blossom green), a term used to describe jadeite of a brilliant emerald-green colour with very dark green spots or veins.

A Pair of Diamond Pendant Earrings

St Moritz SF102,500
(£43,803; $71,678) 20.11.99

These earrings are a striking contemporary design of furling ribbons encrusted with tiny circular diamonds, from which are suspended an undulating fringe of briolette diamonds.

OPPOSITE

A Gold Necklace in Archaeological Revival Style and Matching Earrings

Probably by Melillo, *c.* 1880
London £18,975 ($29,791)
30.VI.99

The design of this gold fringed necklace is almost an exact reproduction of a stunning Etruscan example from the 5th century BC, now kept in the Naples Archaeological Museum. The necklace is designed as a woven band supporting a fringe of pendants in the shape of lotus flowers, acorns, satyr masks and palmettes connected by fine gold chains interspersed with rosette motifs. The clasps are decorated with frogs and floral motifs and the matching earrings are designed as circular shields adorned with Medusa heads.

A Diamond Tiara/Necklace

c. 1890
London £37,800 ($63,126)
3.XII.98

The design of this piece of jewellery, a line of square collet links supporting a fringe made from graduated rows of upright and radiating cushion-shaped diamonds, is called *kokoshnik*. Based on the Russian headdress of the same name, it can be worn either in the hair or around the neck.

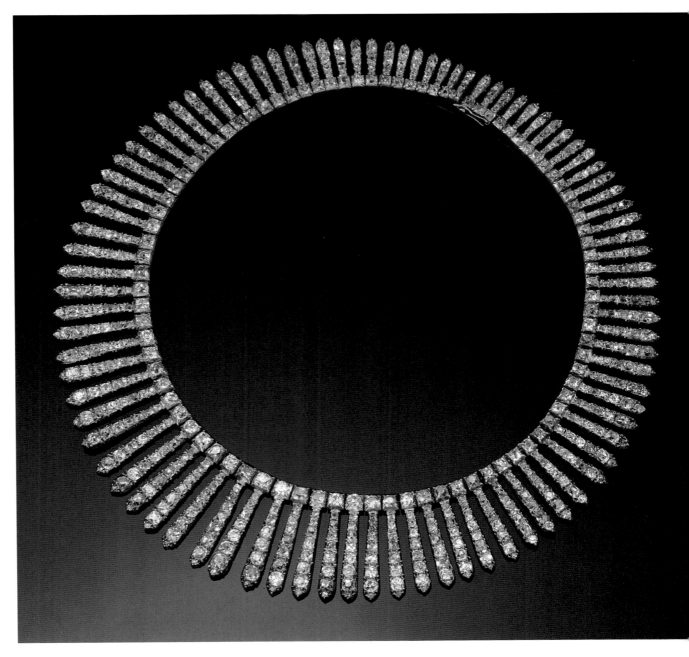

'Tree of Life', by Salvador Dalí: an 18-carat Gold Sapphire and Diamond Necklace
St Moritz SF74,750 (£31,944; $52,272) 20.11.99

Like a number of 20th-century artists, Salvador Dalí investigated media beyond painting and drawing. His excursions into creating ceramics and jewellery are exemplified magnificently by this 'Tree of Life'. Dalí, working with the New York jewellers Alemany & Ertman, juxtaposes a formal rendition of leaves and branches with the playful abstraction of the pendant face creating a fertile and surreal manifestation of his artistic vision.

A Gold, *Plique-à-jour* Enamel and Diamond Bracelet
(detail), by Masriera, *c.* 1920
London £21,850 ($34,305)
30.VI.99

Backed with a black velvet ribbon, this bracelet is made from nine rectangular panels, pierced alternately with floral and foliate motifs. It is decorated with blue and white enamel, made using the *plique-à-jour* technique, which is accompanied by rose- and circular-cut diamonds.

A Gem-set and Pearl Brooch

Boucheron, Paris, c. 1950
Geneva SF487,500
(£211,038; $355,839) 19.XI.98

This item made up part of the sale of Rare Jewels and Precious Objects from a Gentleman's Estate, a collection wonderfully illustrating the result of one person's enthusiasm for beautiful objects. The brooch is made up of a ruby, weighing 5.40 carats, and a step-cut sapphire, weighing 6.32 carats, on one tassel. The other is highlighted by an emerald and two French-cut rubies. Both tassels are supported by 18-carat gold triple-rope chains with circular-cut diamonds. The ends of the swirling ribbons are accented with white and pink pearls.

A Sapphire and Diamond Brooch

'Oiseau de Paradis', Cartier, Paris, c. 1950
Geneva SF355,500
(£153,896; $259,489) 19.XI.98

The inaugural Century of Style auction held by Sotheby's Geneva featured among its many exciting lots this brooch by Cartier. The sale was divided into sections corresponding to periods of this century. The Cartier brooch was part of the 1940s to 1950s section. It is remarkably similar to a brooch that was created for the Duchess of Windsor in 1946, months before the theft of her jewels from Ednam Lodge, Sunningdale.

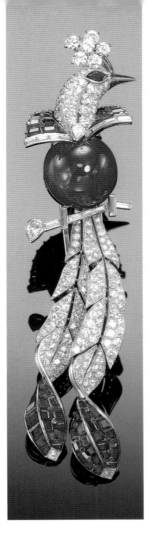

A Fuchsia Diamond Brooch

Orisa, 1950s
Milan L18,400,000
(£6,157; $9,930) 2.VI.99

The original owner of this brooch was Margherita Carosio, one of Italy's leading coloratura sopranos from the 1930s to 1950s. Born in Genoa in 1908 she debuted in 1926 at Novi Ligure in *Lucia di Lammermoor* and thereafter made regular appearances at Covent Garden and La Scala. This particular brooch was designed by Orisa. Her real name was Anna Bacchelli and she worked in a small studio in Piazza Carlo Alberto, Turin. She designed items for many of the major Italian families, including the Royal Family. The piece is pictured upon the score of *Nerone* by Mascagni, which the composer presented to Margherita Carosio.

A Diamond 'White Lilacs' Clip-brooch

Signed *Verdura*
New York $354,500
(£209,155) 20.X.98
From the Estate of Lydia B. Mann

Set in platinum and designed as a flexible, cascading cluster of lilacs, this brooch is set with 21 pear-shaped diamonds weighing approximately 43.25 carats and 29 round diamonds weighing approximately 14.00 carats, topped by a curling leaf and curving branch. The leaf is pavé-set with approximately 237 round diamonds and the branch is set with 29 baguette diamonds, altogether weighing approximately 12.65 carats.

CLOCKS AND WATCHES

A Massive Gold Openface Button Minute Repeating Grande and Petite Sonnerie Clockwatch with Carillon, Dual Up and Down Indicators, Perpetual Retrograde Calendar, Ages and Moon Phases Carriage Watch
c. 1927, Patek Philippe & Co., Geneve, no. 198052
Diameter 6 cm (2⅜ in)
New York $794,500
(£492,590) 15.VI.99

Among the most complicated watches made by Patek Philippe, this example was commissioned by the great watch collector and New York banker Henry Graves, Jr. As an active patron, Mr Graves encouraged the making of watches with an increasing number of complications, creating a newfound market for such pieces.

A Platinum Openface One Minute Tourbillon Watch
c. 1943, Patek Philippe and Co, Geneve, no. 198427
Diameter 5.3 cm (2⅛ in)
New York $453,500
(£281,170) 15.VI.99

Also from Mr Graves's collection, this watch reflects its owner's fascination with the mechanical beauty and technical advantages of the tourbillon mechanism. It won first prize in the Geneva Astronomical Observatory Timing Contest of 1946.

A Belgian Régence Carved Gilt Oak Musical Quarter Chiming Longcase Clock
Gilles de Beefe, Liège, *c.*1740
Height 304 cm (9 ft 11¾ in)
Amsterdam Dfl 528,000
(£159,036; $257,560)
19.IV.99

In setting both a world auction record for a Belgian clock and a Dutch auction record for any clock this remarkable timepiece well exceeded its pre-sale estimate. The maker, Gilles de Beefe, was born into a well-known clockmaking family in 1694. He worked on commissions in Portugal and, on his return to the Low Countries in 1738, received an exclusive patent for making and selling his clocks *'au pays de Liège et Comptè de Looz'*. It was around this time that he constructed this longcase clock for the Comte de Horion.

A Gold Split Second Chronograph Wristwatch with Register and Tachometer

c. 1941, Patek Philippe & Co., Geneve, no. 863725, ref. 1436
Diameter 3.3 cm (1¼ in)
Geneva SF157,500
(£65,353; $105,000) 18.V.99

The reference 1436 was introduced in 1938 and was in production until 1971. Two types of mechanisms were used for this model to activate the split second hand. Earlier pieces, as in the present work, were fitted with a three-functioning winding crown; the later version incorporated a stem mounted split button.

A Gold Perpetual Calendar Chronograph Wristwatch with Moonphases

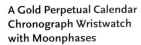

c. 1950, Patek Philippe & Co., Geneve, no. 867733, ref. 1518
Diameter 3.5 cm (1¼ in)
Hong Kong HK$1,208,000
(£96,640; $156,072)
27.IV.99

This 18-carat-gold watch has a nickel-lever movement and 23 jewels. The silvered matte dial has applied baton numerals and two subsidiary dials indicating constant seconds and registers for 30 minutes. It has apertures for month and day in Italian and the date combined with moonphases. The case, dial and movement are signed, and the watch has an 18-carat-gold Patek Philippe buckle.

A Triple Colour Gold Musical Automaton Virgule Watch

Pierre Morand, 1783–89
Diameter 5.2 cm (2⅛ in)
London £24,150 ($41,055)
1.X.98

The glazed back of this watch reveals a triple colour gold harbour scene with five figures in various pursuits and an automaton schooner in full sail dipping through the waves, which is activated by depressing the pendant. Little is known of the maker, beyond the fact that he was based in Paris.

A Stainless Steel and Pink Gold Hooded Bracelet Watch, Rolex Oyster, Chronometre

c. 1935, Chronometrie Beyer, Zurich, ref. 3263
Diameter 3 cm (1¼ in)
Geneva SF44,850 (£18,610; $29,900) 18.V.99

This watch is one of many forgotten pieces discovered by chance at the premises of Chronometrie Beyer in Zurich during recent construction work. The Beyer family firm of watchmakers spans seven generations and, since its foundation in 1760, has passed from father to son.

A Silver Grande Sonnerie and Perpetual Calendar Carriage Clock

Jump, London, hallmarked 1883
Height 16 cm (6½ in)
London £100,500 ($168,840) 17.XII.98

The hump back clocks made by Joseph Jump and his descendants were inspired by the similarly shaped clocks produced by Breguet and James Ferguson Cole. This clock is believed to be the one referred to in letters from Arthur Huyton Jump to the Goldsmith's Co., which identify it as the first and most complicated clock of its kind made by the family firm.

SILVER

A Gold Torah Crown Set with Jewels
European, c. 1825
Height 17.8 cm (7 in),
diameter 12.7 cm (5 in)
New York $1,322,500
(£819,950) 16.111.99

This crown is one of the most important pieces of Judaica to have reached the market in several decades. Its base band has three ovals applied with diamond Hebrew initials standing for the Mishnaic expression used on Torah ornaments '(C)rown of (T)orah, (C)rown of (P)riesthood, (C)rown of (K)ingship' (Mishnah Avot 4:13). The exceptionally high quality of workmanship suggests that it may have been made in Vienna or possibly Russia. It was most likely made as a gift from a supporter or admirer of Rabbi Israel Ruzhin (1797–1850), known as the Ruzhiner Rebbe. Ruzhin saw no conflict between wealth and spirituality and lived in a magnificent palace in Sadgora or Sedigura in Bukovina (Galicia) where he was visited by thousands seeking his insight on spiritual matters. This crown achieved a world auction record for a piece of non-manuscript Judaica.

Two Pairs of Regency Silver Soup Tureens, Covers, Liners and Stands
Paul Storr for Rundell, Bridge & Rundell, London, 1817
Fully marked, numbered and stamped 93, the bases also stamped with the Latin signature of Rundell, Bridge & Rundell

22,734 g (731 oz), length of stands over handles 58.4 cm (23 in); 19,282 g (620 oz), length of stands over handles 50.8 cm (20 in)
New York $739,500 (£458,490) and $635,000 (£393,700) 14.IV.99

Made by Paul Storr after a design attributed to E. Hodges Bailey, these two pairs of tureens, one pair slightly smaller than the other, display the arms of Talbot impaling Lambart. They were made for Charles, 2nd Earl Talbot and 4th Baron, KG (1777–1849) and his wife Frances Thomasine,

eldest daughter of Charles Lambart of Beau Parc, Co. Meath, Ireland. The couple were married in 1800. The family's coat of arms appears both on the tureens and stands, while the *bombé* oval tureen covers are topped with heraldic finials of a lion *passant* standing a cap of maintenance.

**A German Silver-gilt
Mounted Painted Wood
Buttenman**
Early 17th century
Height 23.8 cm (9⅜ in)
Geneva SF102,500
(£44,565; $74,870) 16.XI.98

Carved wood figures
adopting this pose were
popular as drinking vessels
in the wine-producing guilds
Rebleutezünften of South
Germany, Switzerland and
Alsace. This example bears
the maker's mark of a
rampant lion and device to
sinister, and a town mark of a
unicorn to dexter.

**A German Parcel-gilt Silver
Figure of a Huntsman**
Leonhard Han, Konstanz,
early 17th century
Height 35 cm (14 in)
London £177,500 ($289,325)
11.11.99
From the Rothschild and
Rosebery Collection,
Mentmore

The outfit worn by this
huntsman can be seen in
16th-century German prints
such as *The Peasants' Feast*
by Hans Beham and in
hunting prints of pikemen on
foot. This figure wears a
pleated hunting frock,
stockings – one of which is
frayed, a cowl and a
detachable cap bearing an
ibex badge and feather.

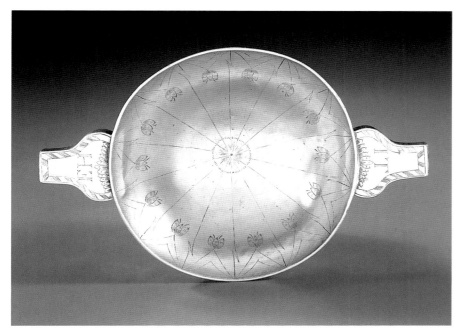

A Scottish Provincial Quaich
William Scott the Elder, Banff or Aberchirder, 1680–1701
Diameter 14 cm (5½ in), weight 202 gr (6 oz, 10 dwt)
London £55,400 ($91,964)
12.XI.98

The dating of this piece is problematic on the basis of the mark, as different authorities suggest different dates for William Scott's working life in Banff. However, it must pre-date his death, which is thought to be 1701. Seventeenth-century Banff silver is of extreme rarity: Sir Charles Jackson lists only two beaker-shaped communion cups in *English Goldsmiths and Their Marks*.

A George I Octafoil Salver
John White, London, 1720, Britannia Standard
Diameter 36.5 cm (14 in), weight 1825 gr (58 oz 14 dwt)
London £56,500 ($90,400)
8.VI.99

John White advertised himself as undertaking engraving 'in the best manner with good despatch at reasonable prices' and, indeed, silver bearing his mark is noted not only for high quality but also for fine engraving. The arms in the centre of this salver are those of Salusbury, probably for John Salusbury of Bachegraig, Denbighshire (d.1762).

MINIATURES AND VERTU

The Cardinal Rampolla Presentation Snuff Box
Jewelled two-colour gold and enamel
Fabergé, maker's mark in full, workmaster Michael Perchin, St Petersburg, 1896–1902, inventory number: 1200
Width 8.9 cm (3½ in)
Geneva SF938,500
(£407,309; $675,179)
17.XI.98

With its miniature of Emperor Nicholas II by Alexei Blaznov, this snuff box was presented as a gift to Cardinal Rampolla in 1902. By the late 19th century most European monarchies had ceased to present *boîtes à portrait*, a practice begun in the late 17th century, but in Russia the tradition continued. An Imperial *boîte à portrait* was a symbol of the emperor's favour, and its value reflected both the rank of the recipient and the nature of the service rendered. This particular box was one of the most expensive ever given by Nicholas II.

A *nécessaire à secrets*
Maker's mark apparently *JALC*, perhaps for Aimé-Joseph-Louis Couturier, charge and discharge marks of Eloi Brichard, Paris, 1758
Width 11 cm (4⅜ in)
London £122,500 ($199,675)
11.11.99

Sold as part of the Rothschild and Rosebery Collection (see pages 36–37), the secrets of this box and the good order of its mechanisms are of the utmost rarity. The box, decorated with Japanese lacquer on its panels, is filled with secret compartments lined with green silk; the interior contains a gold pencil and formerly '*un petit bureau à écrire*'; the lid holds portraits of Franz I, Holy Roman Emperor and Maria Theresia by the same hand. One end of the box contains a gold-mounted calendar dated 1759 and the other end two gold ink bottles and a funnel.

A Fabergé Silver, Enamel and Jewelled Desk Clock
Workmaster Michael Perchin, St Petersburg
Marked with Cyrillic initials of workmaster and *88* standard, also with scratched inventory number *6424*, c. 1900
Height 13 cm (5⅛ in)
New York $57,500 (£35,075)
1.XII.98

A wedding gift to Grand Duchess Helen Vladimirovna (1882–1937), this clock is engraved in Cyrillic 'Grand Duchess Helen Vladimirovna, from P.P. and S.P. Durnovo, 16th August 1902'. Its face, bordered with seed pearls, is set in a triangular surround, which is enamelled in pale blue over a sunray background. Three moss agate cabochons are bordered with diamonds.

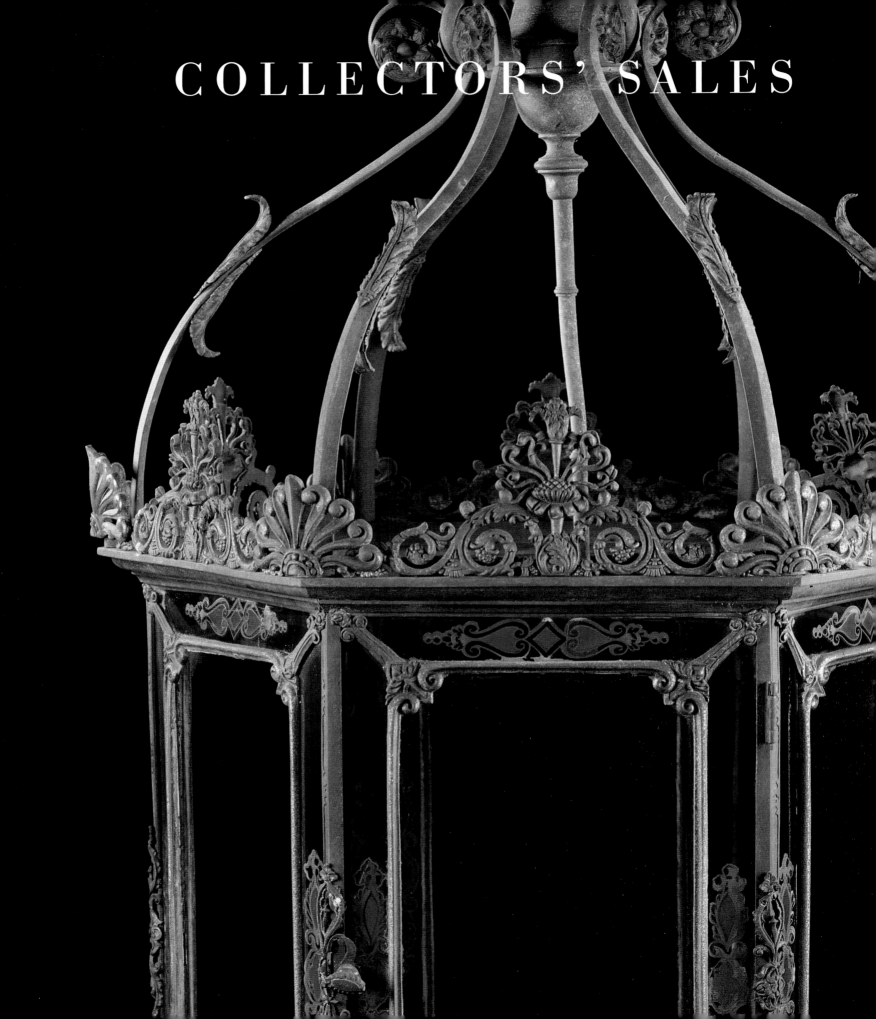

COINS, MEDALS AND STAMPS

Transvaal—Wolmaransstad, 1900 (July) Transvaal pictorial, 1 d. red, S. G. 9
London £4,830 ($7,825)
16.VII.99

The year 1999 was the 100th anniversary of the outbreak of the Boer War, the conflict during which the stamps upon this letter were issued. These stamps are a great rarity of Anglo-Boer philately and especially so on an

envelope; of those recorded the majority were for local use within Wolmaransstad in northern South Africa; very few are recorded beyond the town boundaries. The letter is addressed to the vendor's grandfather, who served with the British Army in South Africa.

1c–10c Louisiana Purchase, 1904
New York $24,150 (£14,490)
22.IX.98

Still in fresh condition, this set consists of five complete panes of 50 stamps, each including an imprint and plate number block of six at the top. The stamps were issued for the 1904 St Louis World's Fair, which itself celebrated the centenary of

the Louisiana Purchase of December 1803. In a secret agreement in 1800 Spain gave a tract of land west of the Mississippi to France; it was then bought by the United States for $15 million in the Louisiana Purchase, thereby doubling the national domain. The final boundaries of the region were not settled for years, but the approximate area is shown on the 10c value.

The Indian Mutiny Victoria Cross, G.C.B. Group awarded to General Sir John Watson, 1st Punjab Cavalry, late 1st European Fusiliers, Founder of Watson's Horse
London £89,500 ($145,885)
11.V.99

This group was sold with a manuscript diary covering all Watson's campaigns, signed on the frontispiece 'John Watson, 14th April 1887'. The diary was a personally edited volume of his campaign diaries. With it were three photographs and a telegram from George V to Watson's son on Watson's death in 1919. Watson was born in Essex in 1829 and began his long military career in Bombay in 1848. He was the founder of the 13th Bengal Lancers, known as Watson's Horse.

Gold Certificate, Twenty Dollars, 1863
New York $396,000 (£249,480) 25.VI.99
Property from the Elizabeth Waldron Estate

This note was discovered in 1998; it is one of only five known to exist of 48,000 originally issued. The vast majority of the notes were withdrawn from circulation and by 1895 only nine were

outstanding. These Certificates of the First Issue were among the earliest Federal banknotes authorized and were the first gold certificates produced by the US government.

Umayyad, dirham, struck at Jiroft,
AH 82 (AD 701)
2.74 g
London £99,000 ($157,410) 27.V.99

Jiroft, in the southern Kirman district of Iran, was not previously known to have struck coins during the Umayyad period. The price achieved was a world auction record for an Islamic silver coin.

1980 (13 September) Exhibition of the People's Republic of China in the United States, commemorative sheetlets of 12 stamps, 8f. and 7of.
Hong Kong HK$2,220,000 (£177,600; $288,600)
12.XI.98

Between 13th September and 21st December 1980 China

staged a series of cultural exhibitions in the US. Each had a 'special' branch of the Peking post office installed. In addition to the regular commemorative issue a special souvenir sheet of 12 stamps was issued for each value. This lot of 1,000 'sheetlets' is probably the largest single holding ever offered for public sale.

中華人民共和國展覽會 EXHIBITION OF THE PEOPLE'S REPUBLIC OF CHINA

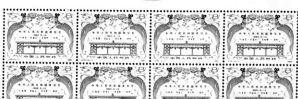

ARMS, ARMOUR AND SPORTING GUNS

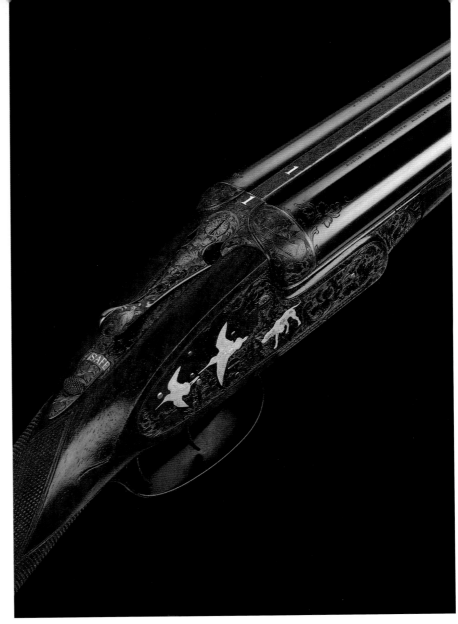

J. Purdey & Sons, a pair of Ken Hunt engraved 12-bore self-opening sidelock ejector guns, nos. 27405/6 (one illustrated)
Gleneagles Hotel £100,500 ($168,840) 31.VIII.98

These guns were built in 1967 and were sold with a copy of a letter from Purdey's Managing Director stating that they were: 'one of the best pairs of guns I have ever built'. The left locks are inlaid with gold pheasants and a gundog and the right locks with a gold dog flushing a brace of snipe. All the locks are signed *K. C. Hunt*, who is one of the most popular gun engravers.

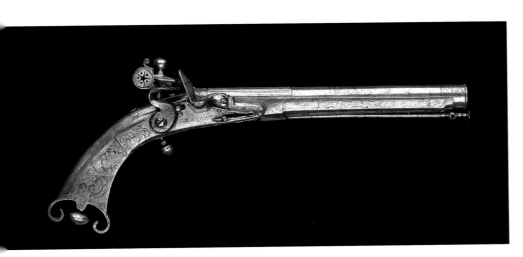

A Scottish Flintlock Belt Pistol
Made entirely of steel and inlaid with silver, by Thomas Caddell, Doune, *c*.1710
Sussex £17,250 ($26,740) 13.VII.99

The distinctive style of the silver inlays, with scrolling Celtic foliage over the breech and hearts, roundels and rectangular panels on the stock, would suggest that this pistol was made by Thomas Caddell the Third. Scottish pistols of this quality and in this condition are extremely rare.

MUSICAL INSTRUMENTS

A Double Bass by Domenico Montagnana
Venice, *c.* 1747
Length of back 117 cm (46 in)
London £155,500 ($251,910)
16.III.99

This double bass was sold accompanied by an article from *The Strad* written in April 1911, which recalls the work of Montagnana and the history of this instrument in particular. The article's author, Towry Piper, describes the instrument as 'in a fine state of preservation', and concludes his enthusiastic outline with: 'Altogether a superb bass with a tone worthy of its imposing exterior.' The price for this instrument represents an auction record for a double bass.

A 'Portable Grand' Pianoforte by John Isaac Hawkins
London, *c.* 1805
Width 103.5 cm (3 ft 4¾ in)
London £20,700 ($34,362)
4.XI.98

This is one of three existing 'portable grand' pianos made by Hawkins, the first English maker of the true upright piano. The instrument is not datec, although it is inscribed with Hawkins's name, and has a silver plaque inside the lid reading: 'This Ancient Piano was made by Thomas Sheraton in 1790 and became the property of Lord Byron when at Newstead Abbey where it remained until his demise in 1824.' All the connections on the plaque have recently been revealed as fictitious.

WINE

**Château Mouton
Rothschild 1945 CB and
Château Mouton
Rothschild 1944 CB**
London £52,800 ($83,952) &
£7,150 ($11,368) 23.VI.99

These two cases of
immaculate provenance had
lain undisturbed in a private
cellar in the Bordeaux region
since their acquisition and
had never been opened until
inspected by Sotheby's. At
auction the particularly
remarkable 1945 vintage
almost doubled its high
estimate of £28,000.

**The Unique Millennium
Superlot from the Cellar of
George Zicarelli**
New York $288,500
(£178,870) 22.V.99

George Zicarelli has
collected some of the
greatest wines made this
century and decided to sell
this spectacular parcel in the
run-up to the millennium
celebrations. The 17 cases
included five of Romanée
Conti 1990, a wine that sold
out so rapidly on its release
that it would be almost
impossible to accumulate
this quantity today and one
of Château Pétrus 1990,
described by Sotheby's
Serena Sutcliffe as 'quite
simply, overwhelming'. The
other wines were Château
Haut Brion 1989, Krug, Clos
du Mesnil 1985 and
Montrachet 1992.

CARS AND AUTOMOBILIA

Frederick Gordon Crosby
The World Land Speed Record Sunbeam at Brooklands, 1922
Watercolour over charcoal heightened with gouache, signed, 47 by 74 cm (18½ by 29⅛ in)
Brooklands Museum £15,927 ($24,846) 16.VII.99

The 12-cylinder Sunbeam pictured here was one of the most famous – and fastest – cars of its day. Early in its career, at the Brooklands track where this painting was sold, it recorded 140.51 mph; later, in the hands of Malcolm Campbell, it recorded the world's flying kilometre record of 150.863 mph.

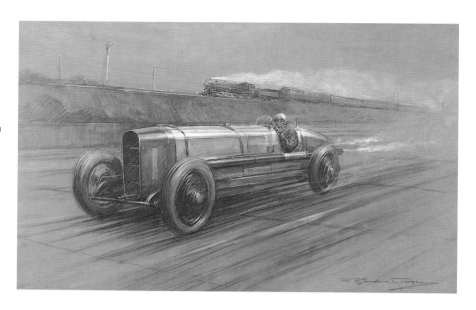

1926 Rolls-Royce Doctor's Drophead Coupé with Dickey
Coachwork by Mullion
London £28,520 ($45,917) 9.IV.99

Doctor's Coupé coachwork enjoyed a considerable vogue and was seemingly so called after medical practitioners found the generally high build, upright lines and ease of entry a particular advantage. The interior contains concealed and secure pill boxes and bespoke door handles; in addition there is a twin-action dickey seat behind the driving compartment.

GARDEN STATUARY

A Stoneware Fountain by Garnkirk

Stamped *Garnkirk*, Scottish, c. 1870
196 by 274 cm (108 by 105 in)
Sussex £106,000 ($169,600)
25.V.99

The Garnkirk Fireclay Company operated between 1838 and 1895, when its fireclay pits were exhausted. It seems that the factory was originally intended to manufacture utilitarian items such as firebricks, but the light stone colour of the fireclay made it suitable for sculpture and pottery. In 1851 the factory is recorded as exhibiting 'glazed wares' in the Great Exhibition at Crystal Palace. This fountain was originally set up at Waternish House (formerly Fasach House) on the Isle of Skye, and at this auction achieved a record as the most expensive garden ornament in Europe.

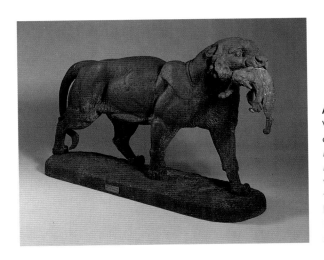

A Cast-iron Figure of a Tiger

Val D'Osne, Paris, late 19th century, plaque impressed
FONDERIES D'ART DU VAL D'OSNE/38 RUE VOLTAIRE/PARIS
137 by 264 cm (4 ft 6 in by 8 ft 8 in)
New York $33,350 (£21,011)
23.VI.99

This tiger, carrying its young in its mouth, steps forward on a naturalistically cast base, set with a plaque. The figure can be dated to post 1870 from the information on the plaque, as Barbezeat & Cie, one of the two primary French manufacturers of art castings in cast-iron from the second half of the 19th century, changed its name to the Société Anonyme du Val d'Osne in 1870. The company based many of their wares on the work of André, whose atelier they took over in 1855.

COLLECTIBLES

Vivien Leigh's dress for her role as Scarlett O'Hara in *Gone With The Wind*, 1939
New York $90,500 (£56,110)
12.VI.99

Scarlett O'Hara's orchid percale dresses are perhaps the most recognizable costumes from *Gone With The Wind*, since this style of dress was on the screen for more than an hour. They figure prominently in some of the greatest moments of the film including the Atlanta hospital scene, searching for Dr Meade to deliver Melanie's baby, the birthing of the baby, the sensational burning of Atlanta sequence, Scarlett sinking to her knees in the fields of Tara as she swears she will never go hungry again, and finally the scene when she tears down the green portières at Tara. Because of the deliberate distressing of the dresses by the costume department, it is a wonder any of them survived. This dress has an unusual bias label marked *ESCAPE Through the fire and McDonough road*.

Frank R. Paul Original Cover Artwork for *Science Wonder Quarterly*, Winter 1930
60.3 by 44.5 cm (23¾ by 17½ in)
New York $76,750 (£48,352)
29.VI.99
From the Sam Moskowitz Collection of Science Fiction

Frank R. Paul is universally recognised as the father of all modern science fiction artwork. Arthur C. Clarke said of him, 'The very first science fiction magazine I ever saw had a cover by Frank Paul – and it is one of the most remarkable illustrations in the history of science fiction, as it appears to be a clear example of precognition on the part of the artist!' This futuristic cover from *Science Wonder Quarterly*, a publication which had many covers by Paul in the 1930s, can be said to be a masterpiece from the golden era of science fiction magazines.

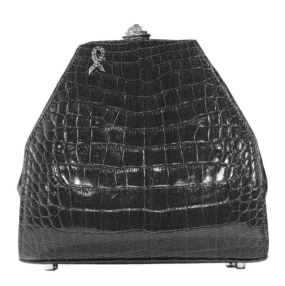

The 'Portrait of Hope' Handbag
New York $11,500 (£7,015)
9.XII.98

Handcrafted from ruby-glazed, American alligator, this bag was designed by Marcia Sherrill of Kleinberg Sherrill especially for Sotheby's To Have and To Hold fashion handbag auction. The proceeds from its sale were donated to the National Alliance of Breast Cancer Organizations (NABCO). Featuring an 18-carat gold clasp set with rock crystal, diamonds and a cabochon ruby, this bag also included a miniature 18-carat gold Breast Cancer insignia inlaid with 16 pink diamonds.

King Kong, 1933
RKO style A three-sheet poster
Lithography art by S. Barret McCormick and Bob Sisk, 206 by 104 cm (81 by 41 in)
New York $244,500 (£151,540) 16.IV.99

A vintage movie poster from David O. Selznick's 1933 classic *King Kong*, this depicts one of the best known images in American film. *King Kong* scooped a handsome price and received a round of applause as the hammer fell after heated competition between two telephone bidders. It secured the second highest price ever paid at auction for a movie poster after *The Mummy* sold for $453,500 in New York in 1997. The *King Kong* poster was purchased by Cecelia Presley, granddaughter of famed director Cecil B. DeMille, and will be donated to the Academy of Motion Picture Arts and Sciences Foundation.

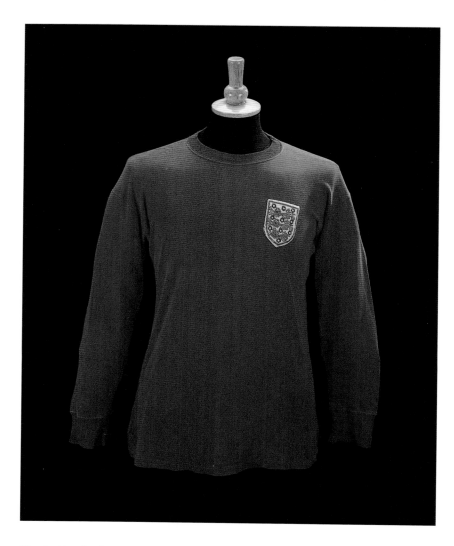

The 'Union Jack' Dress worn by former Spice Girl Geri Halliwell for the Brit Awards, 1997, made by her sister Karen Davis
London £41,320 ($69,417)
16.ix.98

Sold as part of the Rock and Roll Memorabilia sale in London, this dress is one of the trademark items worn by Geri Halliwell during her time with the band The Spice Girls. The dress, along with 88 other pieces of Geri's costumes, was sold to benefit Sargent Cancer Care for Children, raising a total of £146,511 ($246,138).

The Red England No.21 International Jersey Worn by Roger Hunt in the World Cup Final at Wembley, 30 July 1966
London £17,250 ($28,117)
23.11.99

Roger Hunt, who played as a forward in the 1966 World Cup Final, exchanged this shirt with Wolfgang Weber, the West German number 6 whose final-minute equalizing goal forced the match into extra time, although England eventually won. Roger Hunt, whose club football was for Liverpool, played in all six of England's 1966 World Cup matches and scored a total of three goals.

An Edmund Culpeper Compound Monocular Microscope

English, c. 1730
Height of instrument
35 cm (14 in)
London £41,100 ($69,048)
28.x.98

The eyepiece for this microscope is mounted on a circular box containing four objectives of different magnifications. The case is of oak and has a small drawer for specimens and slides. A trade label is applied to the inside of the box with an emblem of crossed daggers and an inscription that reads: 'Edmund Culpeper at the Black and White House, the Sign of the Cross Daggers, in Middle Moorfields, London. Maketh all sorts of Mathematical Instruments in Silver, Brass, Ivory and Wood; also the best Setts of Double and Single Microscopes, Telescopes, Spectacles, Reading Glasses, all Sorts of Convex and Concave Glasses, Quadrants, Fore-Staffs, Gunter-Scales and all other instruments proper for Sailors, at reasonable prices.'

A George II Wooden Doll

English, c.1740
Height 55 cm (21¾ in)
London £32,200 ($51,520)
25.v.99

The exceptionally fresh and original condition of this doll is due to its having been stored in a cupboard in an English country house for generations. The family has inhabited the same residence since 1620 and tradition holds that the doll has been there since she was made. The dress is original with some later additions and the bonnet of ivory silk is extremely rare.

HOUSE SALES

Derwydd Mansion, Carmarthenshire

There have been no major house sales in Wales since Sotheby's sold Penpont in October 1991, but the September 1998 sale of the contents of Derwydd provoked equal enthusiasm among buyers. Tucked away in the green hills of Carmarthenshire, Derwydd was the ancestral home of the Stepney Gulstons, who had connections with the Vaughans, Bevans and Lloyds, as well as being the last remaining connection in Britain to the descendants of van Dyck. The catalogue and sale covered the whole span of the family's history from the 16th century up to the present day. Included were significant works of art, such as the Cotes portrait of Joseph Gulston, which has subsequently entered the J. Paul Getty Museum in Malibu, California, as well as delightful oddities, such as the now-empty portfolio once filled with Joseph Gulston's collection of Rembrandt's works.

Francis Cotes, RA
Portrait of Joseph Gulston (1741–86) and His Brother John Gulston (1750–64)
Signed *F Cotes pinx.1754*
Pastel, in original carved gilt wood frame, 67.5 by 83 cm (26½ by 32½ in)
Carmarthenshire £45,500 ($76,440) 15.IX.98

A 'Famille-rose' Armorial Dinner, Tea and Coffee Service
Qianlong, *c.* 1750, with the arms of Stepney with Vaughan or Lloyd in pretence and the crest of Stepney
Carmarthenshire £85,100 ($142,968) 15.IX.98

Two Silver and Red Leather Dog Collars
English, *c.* 1810, one inscribed *Miss. Gulston-Stepney, 26 Palace Gardens Kensington* together with a watercolour of three pet dogs by Eliza Gulston-Stepney
Carmarthenshire £1,495 ($2,511) 15.IX.98

Noseley Hall, Leicestershire

The two-day house sale at Noseley Hall in Leicestershire drew enormous crowds, both to the view and to the sale. The resulting auction proved to be a terrific success, and the collection reflected the long history of the Hazlerigg family, who had first established themselves in the county in 1419. They rose to prominence in the 17th century, and General Sir Arthur Hazlerigg was an early supporter of the Puritans, and in particular Oliver Cromwell, during the English Civil War. A fine portrait of Hazlerigg (right) was purchased at the sale by the National Portrait Gallery. The sale also included 'The Cromwell Mirror', a shaving mirror reputedly used by Oliver Cromwell, which had been presented to the family in 1905.

In the 18th century Sir Arthur Hazlerigg extensively rebuilt the house, and it was he who ordered the fine Italian scagliola table, which set an auction record for scagliola in the sale. The novelist Samuel Richardson is supposed to have modelled one of his characters on this jovial, cultivated gentleman.

The house was again remodelled in the early 19th century by Sir Arthur Grey Hazlerigg. His handsome hall lantern (right) was discovered, as happens at house sales, in the outhouse!

Robert Walker
Portrait of General Sir Arthur Hesilrige, 2nd Bt (d. 1661)
Inscribed *Sr Arthur, Hesilrige Bart / Son of Sr Thos / 1640*
Oil on canvas, in a carved wood frame, 124.5 by 99 cm (49 by 39 in)
Leicestershire £78,500 ($134,235) 28.1x.98

'The Cromwell Mirror'
A walnut and fruitwood shaving glass, mid 17th century, label on reverse inscribed *This glass which had been many years in the / possession of Mr Mead of Boxmore, Herts was / given by him to Mr Liddell of Hemel Hempstead, / about the year 1865, and was sold by Mr Liddell's / daughter to Sir Arthur Hazlerigg in 1905. / It is understood to be the authentic shaving / glass used by Oliver Cromwell / The Lord Protector*
Height 44.5 cm (1 ft 5½ in)
Leicestershire £3,680 ($6,292) 28.1x.98

A Gilded Walnut Side Table With an Italian Scagliola Top
The table George II, *c.* 1730, with later embellishments, the vignette monogrammed H.P., 79 by 134.5 cm (2 ft 7 in by 4 ft 5 in)
Leicestershire £232,500 ($397,575) 28.1x.98

A Bronze Hall Lantern
Regency, *c.* 1820
86 by 55 cm (2 ft 9 in by 1 ft 9¾ in)
Leicestershire £23,000 ($39,330) 28.1x.98

PRINCIPAL OFFICERS AND SPECIALISTS

Diana D. Brooks
President and Chief Executive Officer

Deborah Decotis Zoullas
Executive Vice President, Sotheby's Holdings

Richard E. Oldenburg
Chairman, Sotheby's North & South America

John L. Marion
Honorary Chairman, Sotheby's North & South America

William F. Ruprecht
Managing Director, Sotheby's North & South America,
Executive Vice President

John D. Block
Vice Chairman, Sotheby's North & South America,
Head of International Jewellery

Warren P. Weitman, Jr
Vice Chairman,
Director of International Business Development

Henry Wyndham
Chairman, Sotheby's Europe

Robin Woodhead
Chief Executive, Sotheby's Europe,
Executive Vice President, Sotheby's Holdings, Inc

George Bailey
Managing Director, Sotheby's Europe

Princess de Beauvau Craon
Deputy Chairman, Sotheby's Europe,
President, Sotheby's France

David Bennett, FGA
Deputy Chairman, Sotheby's Europe,
Chairman, Sotheby's Switzerland,
Head of International Jewellery

Melanie Clore
Deputy Chairman, Sotheby's Europe

The Hon James Stourton
Deputy Chairman, Sotheby's Europe,
Head of European Business Development

James Miller
Deputy Chairman, Sotheby's UK

Simon Taylor
Deputy Managing Director, Sotheby's Europe

Julian Thompson
Chairman, Sotheby's Asia

Carlton C. Rochell, Jr
Senior Vice President,
Managing Director, China and Southeast Asia,
Worldwide Head of Asian Art

The telephone numbers for Sotheby's offices are: Amsterdam 31 (20) 550 2200; Geneva 41 (22) 908 4800; Hong Kong (852) 2524 8121; London 44 (020) 7293 5000; Milan 39 (02) 2950 01; Munich 49 (89) 291 3151; New York 1 (212) 606 7000; Paris 33 (1) 5305 5305; Sussex 44 (1403) 833 500; Tel Aviv 972 (3) 560 1666; Zurich 41 (1) 226 2200

African & Oceanic Art
Jean G. Fritts,
New York & London

American Decorative Arts & Furniture
Leslie B. Keno,
William W. Stahl, Jr,
Wendell Garrett,
New York

American Folk Art
Nancy Druckman,
New York

American Indian Art
David Roche,
New York

American Paintings, Drawings & Sculpture
Peter B. Rathbone &
Dara Mitchell,
New York

Antiquities
Richard M. Keresey &
R. Seth Bright,
New York & London

Arms & Armour
Jürg A. Meier (Europe),
Zurich
Thomas Del Mar
(UK & USA),
Sussex

Books & Manuscripts
Dr Stephen Roe,
London
David N. Redden,
Selby Kiffer,
New York
Jean-Baptiste de Proyart,
Paris

British Pictures
David Moore-Gwyn
(*to 1850*),
James Miller (*to 1850*),
Henry Wemyss
(*Watercolours*),
Martin Gallon (*Victorian*),
Susannah Pollen
(*20th Century*),
London

Ceramics
Simon Cottle,
London
Christina Prescott Walker,
New York

Chinese Art
James B. Godfrey,
New York
Julian Thompson,
London & Hong Kong
Henry Howard Sneyd &
Colin Mackay,
London

Clocks & Watches
Michael Turner (*Clocks*),
Jonathan Darracott
(*Watches*),
London
Daryn Schnipper,
New York

Coins, Medals & Banknotes
Tom Eden,
James Morton,
London
Paul Song,
New York

Collectibles
Dana Hawkes,
New York
Kerry Taylor,
London

Contemporary Art
Tobias Meyer,
Laura Paulson,
New York
Cheyenne Westphal,
London
Florence de Botton,
Paris
Claudia Dwek,
Milan

English Furniture & Decorations
Simon Redburn,
London
Peter Lang,
William W. Stahl, Jr,
New York

European Works of Art & Sculpture
Alexander Kader,
Elizabeth Wilson,
Diana Keith Neal,
London
Margaret Schwartz
(*to 1830*),
Richard Edwards
(*19th & early 20th century*),
New York

Fashion
Tiffany Dubin,
New York
Kerry Taylor,
London

French & Continental Furniture & Decorations
Phillips Hathaway,
Thierry Millerand,
New York
Mario Tavella,
London
Alexandre Pradère,
Paris
Thomas Boller,
Zurich

Garden Statuary & Architectural Items
Jackie Rees,
Sussex
Elaine Whitmire,
New York

Glass & Paperweights
Simon Cottle,
London
Lauren K. Tarshis,
New York

Impressionist & Modern Art
David Norman,
Charles S. Moffett,
John L. Tancock,
New York
Melanie Clore,
Philip Hook,
Michel Strauss,
London
Andrew Strauss,
Paris

Indian & Southeast Asian Art
Carlton C. Rochell, Jr,
New York & London

Islamic Art
Marcus Fraser
(*Manuscripts & Paintings*),
Nicholas Shaw
(*Works of Art*),
London
Richard M. Keresey
(*Works of Art*),
New York

Japanese Art
Neil Davey,
Max Rutherston,
London
Ryoichi Iida,
Sachiko Hori,
New York

Jewellery
John D. Block,
Hoda Esphahani,
New York
David Bennett,
Geneva
Alexandra Rhodes,
Jonathan Condrup,
London
Lisa Hubbard,
Hong Kong

Judaica
Rivka Saker,
Tel Aviv
David N. Redden (*Books*),
Kevin Tierney (*Silver*),
New York
Camilla Previté,
London

Korean Works of Art
Henry Howard-Sneyd,
London
Ryoichi Iida,
New York
Jiyoung Koo,
New York & Korea

Latin American Art
Isabella Hutchinson,
New York

Musical Instruments
Tim Ingles,
London & New York

**19th Century European
Furniture & Works of Art**
Jonathan Meyer,
London
Elaine Whitmire,
New York

**19th Century European
Paintings & Drawings**
Adrian Biddell,
London
Benjamin Doller,
Nancy Harrison,
New York
Eveline van Oirschot,
Amsterdam
Pascale Pavageau,
Paris
Irene Stoll,
Zurich

**Old Master Paintings &
Drawings**
George Wachter,
Christopher Apostle,
New York
Alexander Bell,
Julien Stock,
London
Gregory Rubinstein
(*Drawings*),
London
Nicolas Joly,
Paris

**Orders, Decorations
& War Medals**
Edward Playfair,
London

Oriental Manuscripts
Marcus Fraser,
London
Carlton C. Rochell, Jr,
New York

Photographs
Philippe Garner,
London
Denise Bethel,
New York

Portrait Miniatures & Vertu
Gerald Hill,
New York
Haydn Williams,
London
Heinrich Graf von Spreti,
Munich

Postage Stamps
Richard Ashton,
London
Robert A. G. A. Scott,
New York

Pre-Columbian Art
Stacy Goodman,
New York
Fatma Turkkan-Wille,
Zurich

Prints
Mary Bartow
(*19th & 20th century*),
Nancy Bialler
(*Old Master*),
Christopher Gaillard
(*Contemporary*),
New York
Jonathan Pratt,
London

Rugs & Carpets
Jonathan Wadsworth,
London
Mary Jo Otsea,
New York

Russian Works of Art
Alice Milica Ilich,
London
Gerard Hill,
New York

Silver
Kevin L. Tierney,
Ian Irving,
New York
Peter Waldron
(*English*),
Harold Charteris
(*Continental*),
London
Kobus du Plessis,
Paris

Sporting Guns
Adrian Weller,
Sussex

20th Century Applied Arts
Barbara E. Deisroth,
New York
Philippe Garner,
London

Vintage Cars
Julian Shoolheifer,
London & New York

Western Manuscripts
Dr Christopher de Hamel,
FSA,
London

Wine
Serena Sutcliffe, MW,
Stephen Mould,
London
Michael Davis,
Paul Hart,
Chicago & New York

Sotheby's Institute
Diana Keith Neal
(*Chairman*),
Anne Ceresole,
London
Tom Savage,
New York

Tax & Heritage
James Jowitt,
London

Trusts & Estates
Lindsey Pryor,
New York

Valuations
Hon James Stourton,
London
Lindsey Pryor,
New York
Diederik Westerhuis,
Amsterdam

Sotheby's Financial Services
Mitchell Zuckerman,
Shelley Fischer,
Catherine Chiarella,
New York
Ann-Marie Casey-Jones,
London

**Sotheby's International
Realty**
Stuart N. Siegel
(*President*),
New York
Paul Tayler,
London

**Business Development
North & South America**
James G. Niven
New York

**Sotheby's Worldwide
Web Site**
http://www.sothebys.com

INDEX

Acknowledgements

Prices given throughout include the buyer's premium applicable in the saleroom concerned. These prices are shown in the currency in which they were realized. The sterling and dollar equivalent figures, shown in brackets, are based upon the rates of exchange on the day of the sale.

The editor would like to thank Paul Donaher, Jennifer Conner, Tara Heffler, Diane Pia, Sandra Burch, Nick Deschamps, Pari Jablon, Patrick Sheehan and all the Sotheby's departments for their help.